Heinrich Himmler

Titles in the **Holocaust Heroes and Nazi Criminals** *series:*

Adolf Eichmann
Executing the "Final Solution"
0-7660-2575-6

Adolf Hitler
Evil Mastermind of the Holocaust
0-7660-2533-0

Anne Frank
Hope in the Shadows of the Holocaust
0-7660-2531-4

Elie Wiesel
Surviving the Holocaust, Speaking Out Against Genocide
0-7660-2576-4

Heinrich Himmler
Murderous Architect of the Holocaust
0-7660-2532-2

Oskar Schindler
Saving Jews From the Holocaust
0-7660-2534-9

Raoul Wallenberg
Rescuing Thousands From the Nazis' Grasp
0-7660-2530-6

Holocaust Heroes and Nazi Criminals

Heinrich Himmler

Murderous Architect of the Holocaust

Richard Worth

Enslow Publishers, Inc.

40 Industrial Road	PO Box 38
Box 398	Aldershot
Berkeley Heights, NJ 07922	Hants GU12 6BP
USA	UK

http://www.enslow.com

———

To Karen A. Jeffers for all her support in my writing career.

———

Acknowledgments

I wish to acknowledge the help of my father,
Arthur Worth, for instilling in me a love of history,
research, and writing. I also wish to thank
my history professors at
Trinity College, Hartford, Connecticut,
for all the training I received as a historian.

Library of Congress Cataloging-in-Publication Data:

Worth, Richard.
 Heinrich Himmler : murderous architect of the Holocaust / Richard Worth.—1st ed.
  p. cm. — (Holocaust heroes and Nazi criminals)
 Includes bibliographical references and index.
 ISBN 0-7660-2532-2
  1. Himmler, Heinrich, 1900–1945—Juvenile literature. 2. Nazis—Biography—Juvenile literature. 3. War criminals—Germany—Biography—Juvenile literature. 4. Holocaust, Jewish (1939–1945)—Juvenile literature 5. World War, 1939–1945—Atrocities—Juvenile literature. I. Title. II. Series.
 DD247.H46W67 2005
 940.53'18'092—dc22

                                             2004028114

Printed in the United States of America

10 9 8 7 6 5 4 3 2 1

To Our Readers: We have done our best to make sure all Internet addresses in this book were active and appropriate when we went to press. However, the author and the publisher have no control over and assume no liability for the material available on those Internet sites or on other Web sites they may link to. Any comments or suggestions can be sent by e-mail to comments@enslow.com or to the address on the back cover.

Illustration Credits: Courtesy of the Simon Wiesenthal Library and Archives, Los Angeles, Calif., p. 103; Enslow Publishers, Inc., p. 90; National Archives and Records Administration, pp. 10, 12, 20, 24, 44, 61, 78, 88, 92, 105, 140 (third from top), 143 (third from top), 144 (bottom); Reproduced from the Collections of the Library of Congress, pp. 40, 42, 54, 63, 138; USHMM, pp. 7, 8, 36, 57, 85, 121, 135, 140 (top), 140 (second from bottom), 143 (second from bottom), p. 141 (bottom), 145, 153, 155, 158; USHMM, courtesy of Harry Lore, p. 143 (top); USHMM, courtesy of Instytut Pamieci Narodowej, pp. 99, 108, 117, 120; USHMM, courtesy of James Blevins, pp. 16, 29, 31; USHMM, courtesy of James Sanders, p. 141 (top); USHMM, courtesy of Lorenz Schmuhl, 140 (third from bottom), 142 (top), 143 (third from bottom) USHMM, courtesy of Lydia Chagoll, p. 130; USHMM, courtesy of Main Commission for the Prosecution of the Crimes against the Polish Nation, 140 (second from top), 142 (bottom), 143 (second from top); USHMM, courtesy of the National Museum of American Jewish History, 140 (bottom), 143 (bottom); USHMM, courtesy of the State Archives of the Russian Federation, p. 144 (top); National Archives and Records Administration, pp. 10, 12, 20, 24, 44, 61, 78, 88, 92, 105; Reproduced from the Collections of the Library of Congress, pp. 40, 42, 54, 63.

Cover Illustration: USHMM (Himmler Portrait)

Contents

Fast Facts About Heinrich Himmler 9

1   A Meeting at Wannsee 10

2   Early Life and Anti-Semitism 16

3   Becoming a Nazi 31

4   Chief of the German Police 42

5   Persecuting Jews on Germany's Borders 61

6   Killing Jews in Russia 78

7   Architect of the Holocaust 92

8   Himmler Increases the Jewish Terror 105

9   Last Year in Power 120

10   The Legacy of Heinrich Himmler 135

Timeline 140

Chapter Notes 145

Glossary 153

Further Reading and Internet Addresses 155

Index 158

Heinrich Himmler

Fast Facts About Heinrich Himmler

Born: Heinrich Himmler was born in Munich, Germany, on October 7, 1900.

Religion: Himmler was raised as a devout Roman Catholic.

Childhood: As a boy, Himmler was poor at sports, although an above-average student.

Military Service: Himmler trained to serve in World War I, but the war ended before he entered the conflict.

Nazi Membership: During the 1920s, after achieving little success in other fields, Himmler became a member of the Nazi party and the SS. His Nazi membership number was 14,303. Himmler's SS number was 168.

Positions Held: Because of his ruthless efficiency and loyalty to Hitler, Himmler was rapidly promoted from Deputy Reichsführer-SS, to Reichsführer-SS, and then also to Chief of Police by 1936.

Atrocities: During the 1930s, Himmler directed the construction of a variety of concentration camps where Jews as well as political prisoners could be held and killed.

As Germany was losing the war in 1943–1944, Himmler increased his efforts to eliminate the Jewish population.

Betrayal of Hitler: Himmler tried to negotiate a German surrender to the Allies in 1945, but his betrayal was discovered by Hitler, who stripped him of his power.

Death: Himmler committed suicide on May 23, 1945, while in British custody.

1

A Meeting at Wannsee

On January 20, 1942, a group of high-ranking Nazi officials met outside of Berlin, the capital of Germany. The site of the meeting was a plush villa overlooking a lake, the Wannsee. The villa was owned by the Nazi Schutzstaffel (SS). This was the dreaded state security operation of the German Third Reich. The SS was headed by Heinrich Himmler. About a month before the meeting, Himmler had met with the Nazi dictator, Adolf Hitler. On his calendar, Himmler recorded the purpose of the meeting: "Jewish question/to be exterminated as partisans." According to historian Christopher Browning, this meant, "Most likely, they discussed how the killing of the Jews was to be justified and what were the rules for speaking about it."[1]

Since World War II had begun in 1939, Himmler and the SS had led the efforts to kill Jews across Europe. Himmler was not present at the Wannsee meeting; however, it was held with his approval. The conference itself was headed by Himmler's chief of staff, Reinhard Heydrich. Nevertheless, Himmler's shadow loomed over the entire gathering, which simply ratified what he had already begun. This was the Final Solution—the Nazi plan to murder the Jews of Europe.

The gathering of Nazi officials was very short. It lasted only about an hour. The Nazis disguised their words so there would be no record of the fact that they were referring to a murderous Final Solution. During the meeting, Heydrich talked about an order he had received from Hermann Göring, Hitler's second-in-command, on July 31, 1941. This order called for a "total solution" to the Jewish issue in Europe. It probably meant a plan for the murder of all Jews.[2] Himmler had been put directly in charge of executing the Final Solution, under Hitler's direction. Both Himmler and Hitler had long been convinced that Jews were the cause of all the problems that had been faced by Germany for centuries. Indeed, Hitler blamed the Jews for causing Germany's defeat in World War I. Hitler also held them responsible for causing World War II. As he later wrote, they were the "real guilty party in this murderous struggle." He also wanted to make sure that "the real culprits would have to pay for their guilt even though by more humane means than war." By this, Hitler meant killing all of Europe's Jews in gas chambers.[3]

By 1942, Nazi armies had overrun most of Europe. They were, in early January, poised to conquer the Soviet Union. Hitler was especially eager to defeat the Soviets, which he believed were led by Jewish Communists. This final victory would give the Nazis complete control of continental Europe, placing almost 11 million Jews entirely within their power. The Nazi leader, or Führer, planned nothing less than the

By the time of the Wannsee Conference, German forces
were attacking the Soviet Union.

murder of all these Jews. He had put Himmler, as head of the SS, in charge of carrying out this ruthless directive.

Discussions of Wannsee

The Nazis who were gathered at Wannsee discussed the Jewish situation in occupied Europe. Heydrich, acting on behalf of Himmler, pointed out that the Jews had already been driven out of Germany. In fact, they had been forced into concentration camps in the east. Indeed, Heydrich emphasized that the "evacuation of the Jews to the East . . ." was already underway throughout Europe. But, then he added that this was only a stopgap measure on the road to the "future final solution of the Jewish question." Heydrich emphasized that the Nazis intended to be very thorough in rounding up Jews. "In the course of the practical execution of the final solution, Europe will be combed through from west to east."[4]

Heydrich mentioned where these Jews were located. He said that there were almost 3 million in the Ukraine, part of the Soviet Union. There were over 2 million in an area of eastern Poland called the General Government and almost seven hundred fifty thousand in Hungary. Smaller numbers lived in Romania, Finland, France, Holland, and Belgium. In total, Heydrich said there were over 11 million Jews. Led by Heinrich Himmler, the mass destruction of the Jews was already under way. Jews were being rounded up in Lithuania, Poland, and western Europe. Many of them, including old people, women, and children, were taken out to wooded areas and shot.

Others were transported, under Himmler's leadership, into ghettos in major European cities, such as Warsaw, Poland, and Vilnius, Lithuania. Here, many Jews died of starvation. Still others were being taken to death camps at locations such as Chelmno in Poland. These had been established under Himmler's direction. There, the Jews were being killed with lethal gas by the thousands. A few were put to work at concentration camps making war matériel, such as clothing for Nazi soldiers and parts for airplanes and submarines. Eventually, with little to eat and repeated physical punishment from SS guards, these Jews became too weak to work and were murdered.

These facts were never openly mentioned at the Wannsee Conference. However, Adolf Eichmann—one of the SS officers who attended the meeting—later reported that there was no doubt in anyone's mind what they were discussing. The purpose of the Wannsee Conference was to confirm the Final Solution that had already begun across Europe.[5] As Heydrich put it, those Jews who could work would be employed to build roads. This work would be so tough that:

> doubtless a large portion will be eliminated by natural causes. The possible final remnant will, since it will undoubtedly consist of the most resistant portion, have to be treated accordingly, because it is the product of natural selection and would, if released, act as the seed of a new Jewish revival."[6]

After World War II was over, Adolf Eichmann was asked what the phrase "treated accordingly" meant. He answered: "Killed. Killed. Undoubtedly."[7]

The Wannsee Conference was designed to coordinate the massive effort that involved thousands of Nazi SS members and other officials in transporting Jews from locations throughout the continent to places of execution. As historian Martin Gilbert wrote: What had been occurring in a "fragmentary and spasmodic" way, "was to become formal, comprehensive and efficient. The technical services such as the railways, the bureaucracy and the diplomats would work in harmony, towards a single goal."[8]

The conference put the stamp of approval on the genocide. A genocide is the destruction of a specific type of people, in this case the Jews. This was a large part of what became known as the Holocaust—the murder of 11 million people, including 6 million Jews, by the Nazis. The man who has been called the architect of this genocide was Heinrich Himmler.

Early Life and Anti-Semitism

Heinrich Himmler was born on October 7, 1900, in Munich, the capital of Bavaria, a state located in southern Germany. The Himmler family had deep roots in Bavaria. Heinrich's grandfather, Konrad Himmler, had served in the 1st Royal Bavarian Regiment, during the early part of the nineteenth century. After leaving the army, he became a policeman in Munich and later rose to the rank of police station commander in northern Bavaria.

When Konrad Himmler was fifty-three, he married Agathe Rosina Kiene, who was twenty-nine. They lived in Lindau, a city near the border with Switzerland. Here, their son Gebhard—Heinrich Himmler's father—was born in 1865. By this time, Konrad Himmler had left the police force. He served in the Lindau government until he died in 1873.

Bavaria was part of the new German empire. For centuries, the German-speaking world had been made up of a number of independent states. The largest was Bavaria, which had been ruled by the Wittelsbach family since the twelfth century. During the 1860s, some of the states were united by Otto von Bismarck, the chief minister of Prussia. At this time, Prussia and Austria were the most powerful states under Bismarck's rule. Following a victorious war with Austria in 1866, Bismarck forced some of the southern German states to join a confederation led by Prussia. Then in order to wage war against neighboring France in 1870, Bismarck convinced the rest of the German states, including Bavaria, to join Prussia in a large German empire. The empire was formally proclaimed in 1871 after the defeat of France. The new empire was led by Prussia, and its king was called the kaiser. Prince Otto von Bismarck became the chancellor of Germany.

As the power of Germany grew, the importance of the Himmler family increased with it. Gebhard Himmler's mother was very eager for him to be successful. In 1884, he entered the University of Munich. One of the oldest and most prestigious institutions in Europe, it was founded during the fifteenth century. Gebhard Himmler remained at the university for the next ten years, receiving advanced degrees. In 1894, Gebhard began a lifelong career as a professor at a gymnasium—the German equivalent of a high school. Students that graduated from a gymnasium were expected to go to a university. Gebhard also became the personal tutor of Prince Heinrich, the son of Prince Arnulf of Wittelsbach. This gave Gebhard Himmler an important connection to the royal family that still ran the government in Bavaria after it became part of the German empire.

In 1897, while working in Munich, Gebhard married Anna Maria Heyder, the daughter of a successful businessman. The Himmlers had three children—Gebhard, the oldest; Heinrich; and later a third son, Ernst.

Growing Up in Bavaria

When Heinrich was born, Prince Heinrich became the baby's godfather. In a letter to the prince, Gebhard Himmler wrote: "It would perhaps interest you to know, dear Prince Heinrich, that on his second day of existence on this earth, our little offspring weighed seven pounds and 200 grams [8 pounds, 5 ounces] and measured 52 cm [20½ inches]. Thankfully he is lively and always hungry."[1] Two years after Heinrich's birth, his father took a higher-paying job at a gymnasium in Passau, another Bavarian city. Shortly after the family moved there, however, Heinrich was afflicted with a serious illness that may have been tuberculosis. This is a disease of the lungs that is frequently fatal. The Himmlers moved to the countryside, away from Passau, where many people had already contracted tuberculosis. In the country, Heinrich made a steady recovery. As his father wrote Prince Heinrich: "Things are going rather normally for us now, thank God. An examination by the district physician yesterday showed that Heini's healthy condition which has been achieved by so much struggle is holding, with the exception of some spots of remaining infection."[2] During the spring of 1904, Gebhard Himmler decided to accept a new appointment at a gymnasium in Munich, and the family returned to their former home.

Heinrich soon entered elementary school in Munich. His parents had very specific goals for him and his brothers as they grew older. As historian Bradley Smith wrote, these included "to prepare their offspring for careers as professional men with close connections with the court."[3] The court of the Wittelsbachs was the center of power in Bavaria. A close relationship with the court could help the young Himmlers advance in their careers.

As Heinrich grew up, he was a good student. His parents also raised him to be a devout Catholic. However, he was not as strong as many of the other boys, and his poor eyesight forced him to wear glasses. Heinrich was introduced by his father to the same hobbies that he enjoyed. These included stamp collecting and book collecting. In the evenings, the boys listened to stories that Professor Himmler read from books of German history. In addition, he told them about the adventures of their grandfather when he served in the army and later upheld the law as a policeman. The family spent summers in the beautiful Bavarian countryside, hiking and swimming.

About this time, Heinrich began to keep a diary. This was his father's suggestion. Gebhard Himmler was a methodical, well-organized man. The diary enabled Heinrich to keep an organized, detailed account of his life. Here he recorded all the important events of his childhood. In 1911, he wrote: "First swim, Second swim." In all there were thirty-seven of these swims during the summer vacation.[4] Heinrich had become very disciplined about keeping notes of his activities. Although Heinrich was short and not naturally good at athletics, he was trying to develop himself by regular exercise. The gymnasium that Heinrich attended had a regular gymnastics program. However, he was not very good at it. Indeed, the gym teacher regularly made an example of Heinrich in front of the rest of the class. This probably made him feel inferior to his classmates.[5]

World War I

Himmler's diary entries continued in 1914. But during the summer they were overtaken by events in Europe. On June 28, the heir to the Austrian empire, Archduke Franz Ferdinand, was assassinated in Sarajevo, then the capital of Bosnia.

Wolfgang Falk Zipperer

When he was a boy, Heinrich Himmler's closest friend was Wolfgang Falk Zipperer. The two boys went to elementary school together and attended the same gymnasium. Falk Zipperer shared Heinrich's enthusiasm for German participation in World War I and hoped to fight in the battles against the French and English. In April 1917, Zipperer left his studies at the gymnasium to join the Second Bavarian Infantry Regiment. After the war, Zipperer returned to Munich, where he renewed his friendship with Himmler. The two men remained friends during the 1920s and 1930s. In fact, by 1937, Zipperer had become a captain in the SS, the elite military organization of Nazi Germany. The *Reichsführer*, or leader of the SS, was Zipperer's old friend, Heinrich Himmler.

German soldiers shoot from a trench during World War I.

The Bosnians were Slavic people who were part of the Austrian empire. They were allied with their neighbor Serbia in calling for a separate government. A Serb nationalist had assassinated the archduke.

The Austrians were allied with the German empire. After receiving German support, they decided to confront the Serbs. The Austrian government demanded that their officials be permitted to enter Serbian territory to search for any radicals involved in the assassination of the archduke. When Serbia refused, Austria prepared to launch an invasion against the Serbs. The Austrians were backed up by their ally, Germany. On the other side, the Serbs were supported by their ally, Russia. As both sides mobilized, World War I broke out in August 1914. France entered the war on the side of its ally, Russia, while Great Britain joined France. They faced the armies of Germany and Austria.

Himmler and World War I

As the war began, thirteen-year-old Heinrich Himmler recorded the events in his diary. "Mobilization in Germany. . . . Germany declares war on Russia. . . . French and Russian attacks on the borders. . . . England has declared war."[6] Heinrich wanted to join the German navy. However, his poor eyesight made him unqualified for service. During the early stages of the war, German armies poured across the border into Belgium and France. The French armies were driven westward to the outskirts of Paris. In his diary, Heinrich Himmler recorded his delight at these early German victories. Indeed, his diary entries refer to French and Belgian soldiers being "chopped up fast," and the British being "thrashed." Most of the diary does not contain such descriptive words. Himmler's biographer Peter Padfield suggests that these descriptions may be early indications of

21

Himmler's sadistic personality.[7] Sadism means taking pleasure in bringing pain to other people.

In September 1914, the German armies were stopped short of Paris by a spirited French defense at the First Battle of the Marne. As a result of the French victory, the war along the Western Front bogged down into four years of bloody warfare. German trenches on one side faced British and French positions on the other, in a long line of continuous defenses that stretched from the Belgian coast to Switzerland.

Although he was only fourteen, Heinrich Himmler wanted to participate in the war. In 1915, he joined the Jugendwehr, a program for teenagers to begin training for the army. Heinrich also tried to increase his exercise program so he would have the stamina to become a soldier. Meanwhile, during 1915, massive battles raged along the Western Front in Gallipoli, Turkey. During 1916, at Verdun (France) on the Western Front, approximately six hundred eighty thousand soldiers were killed or wounded. Late in 1916, Prince Heinrich, a courageous military officer, was killed in battle. His death was mourned throughout Bavaria. Meanwhile, Gebhard Himmler—Heinrich's older brother—had enlisted in the 2nd Bavarian Infantry and was preparing to go to the front. Heinrich's mother made clothes that were sent to the Bavarian soldiers.

At first, Heinrich Himmler could only obtain a position in the Hilfsdienst, an organization that cared for German widows and orphans. Finally, he was accepted into the 11th Bavarian Infantry Regiment, beginning training in January 1918. This was the first time Heinrich had lived away from home, and he was homesick for his parents. He urged them to write to him as often as possible and asked his mother to send him food and clothes. At one point, Heinrich's regiment received word that it might be called to the front. Although he was eager for battle, Heinrich was also afraid of being killed on the battlefield.[8]

However, he was spared the need to go to the front lines, because his regiment was not called up. Meanwhile, the position of the German armies was growing worse. Early in 1918, they had launched a massive offensive along the Western Front, designed to knock Britain and France out of the war. But the attack had failed. With the help of the United States, which had entered the war a year earlier, British and French soldiers drove the German armies steadily back toward Germany. By September, the war was nearly over. But Heinrich Himmler was still being trained for battle—this time in a machine-gun course. By the time the program ended and Heinrich was ready to head for the front, the German armies had signed an armistice agreement. Meanwhile, the German government had collapsed and the kaiser had abdicated, or left the throne. In November 1918, the war ended. Heinrich had never been given a chance to prove himself in battle. Instead, he was sent home to Munich.

After the War

After the war ended, Heinrich Himmler completed his school education. Meanwhile, a new German government was being established. It was called the Weimar Republic, because the government had been established at Weimar, Germany, after the end of World War I. It was a middle-of-the-road, democratically elected government led by Friedrich Ebert. However, Communists on the left and military leaders on the right believed that the government was not strong enough to rebuild Germany and strengthen it after the defeat in World War I.

Unrest was occurring across Germany. Revolts broke out among German sailors and soldiers. In Bavaria and other German states, volunteer military organizations, called Freikorps, were hastily set up to keep order. They were also intended to defend Germany against a possible takeover by Communists. In 1917, Communists, led by V. I. Lenin, had established a new government in Russia, later renamed the Soviet Union in 1922. Under Communism, private property was eliminated. All property was owned by the central government. The government was run by the Communist party. After the war, Communist groups began to gain influence in other countries outside of the Soviet Union, including Germany. Many Germans feared that Communism might bring an end to the Weimar government and undermine the German economy, which was based on individual ownership of stores, factories, and land.

In Bavaria, a Communist group called the Union of Revolutionary Bavarian Internationalists took control of the government in Munich during 1919. Many leaders of this group were Jewish, according to historian Peter Padfield. This fueled anti-Semitism, a hatred of Jews. According to Padfield, anti-Semitism had been growing in Munich since the nineteenth century. Many German small business owners lost their shops to more successful Jewish merchants.[9]

Soldiers were sent to Munich to put down the revolt. They were joined by organizations of volunteers, called Freikorps. Heinrich Himmler joined the Freikorps Oberland late in April 1919. The Freikorps members believed in the same

Germany was defeated in World War I. Here, German prisoners of war stand in a French camp.

ideas that were later championed by the Nazis. These included a love of Germany and the purity of the German race.[10] Himmler hoped to participate in action with the Freikorps against the Communists. However, once again he was disappointed. By early May, before Himmler could participate, the Communists had been defeated.

Himmler's New Career

After the Communist revolt in Bavaria had ended, Himmler returned to school, where he graduated in 1919. Following graduation, he decided to attend an agricultural school to study agronomy, the science of farming. Before his studies began, however, Himmler went to work on a farm in Bavaria. He wanted to gain some practical experience with farming. His work schedule was grueling. As he wrote in his diary:

> Around 4 a.m. in the horse stall [cleaning it out], then coffee at about 5:30. At 6 the real work begins. So far it has been sheaving [bundling stalks of] grain. At 10:30 in the stall again. At 11:30 lunch. At 12:00 the work begins again, in the field or loading straw. 3–3:30 bread and beer, then work until 6:00. At 6 in the Stall. 6:30 dinner. Then to bed around 8:00.[11]

Through hard work, Himmler was hoping to build up his body and gain strength. As historian Bradley Smith put it: "There is no question that throughout his life he was obsessed by the desire to achieve a fine physique and that he suffered at . . . his softness and awkwardness."[12] This occurred on the farm, just as it had in school, where Himmler had been laughed at because he did not succeed in athletics.

Once again Himmler failed when he tried to demonstrate his physical strength. His strenuous schedule produced a severe illness that forced him to be rushed to the hospital. During his recovery, Himmler read a variety of books that included some that were fiercely anti-Semitic—that is, anti-Jewish. Historians are not sure why he read these books. Apparently, his father was not anti-Semitic. Nevertheless, there was a general anti-Semitism in Bavaria. This had increased during the attempted Communist takeover, that was led by Jews.[13] He agreed with the books' conclusions that the Jews had somehow betrayed Germany and caused the loss of the war. In addition, Himmler believed that Jews had tried to lead a Communist takeover of Bavaria.[14]

After his release from the hospital, Himmler had to give up work on the farm and begin his studies at the agricultural school. Late in 1919, Himmler and his brother Gebhard joined the Fourteenth Alarm Company. This was a reserve unit designed to safeguard Germany from any other revolutions. Himmler wrote: "Today I have put the uniform on again. For me it is always the most precious clothing one can wear."[15]

While Himmler was beginning his career, the victorious Allies were meeting at Versailles, France, to determine the fate of Germany. As a result of the Treaty of Versailles, Germany was forced to admit responsibility for causing World War I. Its army was reduced to only one hundred thousand men. The German government was required to give France the regions of Alsace and Lorraine, located in western Germany. These had been taken from the French during the war in 1870. In addition, the Allies demanded that Germany make reparations—payments for the damage caused during the war. The treaty did not establish the size of the reparations, but called on a commission to do it. Nevertheless, the Allies indicated that the amount would be very high, totaling billions of dollars. It was eventually set at $35 billion.

The German people felt humiliated by the treaty. Himmler believed that only a strong leader like Bismarck could rescue the German nation and lead it back to glory.[16] Indeed, he wanted to participate in this cause. "Perhaps in a few years I'll be involved in war and struggle," he wrote in his diary. "I'd be so happy with a war of liberation, and would go along if I can still move a limb."[17] Himmler joined a fraternity at school and learned how to use a sword. He frequently participated in duels with other students. In these matches, Himmler wore padding and protection over his face. However, his arms were exposed, and he was cut by his opponent. Nevertheless, Himmler was very proud of how well he had performed.[18] All the time, Himmler kept careful notes of his activities in his diary. He was very disciplined about recording all of the important events that occurred each day of his life. He also kept reading anti-Semitic books and writing down his negative attitudes toward the Jews. In his writings, he regularly referred to people as "Jewish louse" or "Jewboy."[19]

Meanwhile, Himmler worried that his studies might be cut short at agricultural school. The German economy had collapsed after the war, and inflation was spiraling out of control. Early in 1919, one American dollar equaled about nine German marks, and it equaled fourteen marks by the middle of the year. It reached 400 to the dollar in 1922[20] and 350,000 to the dollar by 1923. As a result, German families, including the Himmlers, saw their entire savings wiped out. They needed all the money available to them to buy food and clothing. Himmler's father continuously urged him to watch

This picture of Himmler was taken in the late 1920s, during his early days in the Nazi party. A Nazi pin can be seen on his lapel.

his spending while at school. By this time, Heinrich Himmler was completing his course of study at agricultural school, and he had found a job at a fertilizer company.

Himmler's anti-Semitism continued to grow. After reading one book that criticized the Jews, Himmler commented: "These terrible Jews."[21] Himmler continued to participate in the activities of the Fourteenth Alarm Company. At one of their meetings, he met Ernst Röhm. Röhm was a radical leader who wanted to replace the government of Germany, the Weimar Republic, with a new regime led by German soldiers. Early in 1923, Himmler joined a group called the Reichsflagge, led by Röhm. The members of this organization wanted to build a strong Germany that would be ready to take on France and Great Britain in another war. They also felt humiliated by Germany being forced to pay large reparations to the Allies.

In 1923, Germany had received another humiliation at the hands of the French. Since the German government had been unable to pay its war reparations, French troops marched into the Ruhr Valley. This was a highly industrialized, economically powerful part of Germany. Men like Röhm and Himmler were furious at the French for taking over this area and undermining the German economy. Shortly after the French takeover, they joined a larger radical group, called the Nationalsozialistische Deutsche Arbeiterpartei—German National Socialist Workers' Party (NSDAP). The party was founded in 1919. Calling themselves the Nazis, they were led by Adolf Hitler. Among Hitler's strongest beliefs was that the Versailles Treaty had humiliated Germany and should be disregarded by the German government. He also believed that Jews were not entitled to citizenship in Germany. These beliefs appealed to Röhm and Himmler.

3

Becoming a Nazi

In August 1923, Heinrich Himmler became a member of the Nazi party. His membership number was 14,303. About the same time, he quit his job at the fertilizer company and devoted himself to the Nazi cause. Since Himmler earned no money from the party, he was forced to live at home with his parents. They believed that their son had made a big mistake joining the Nazi party, which was a small radical group that seemed out of step with the future of Germany.

In November 1923, however, Hitler made a decision that he hoped many Germans would support. He had already denounced the French for occupying the Ruhr Valley. Hitler also scorned the decision by the Weimar government to make reparation payments in order to convince the French to leave the Ruhr. Many people in Bavaria agreed with Hitler. On the night of November 8, 1923, Hitler addressed a large political rally at a beer hall in Munich. He called on his supporters to take over the Bavarian government. From there, they may have hoped to March on Berlin, the German capital, and take control of the government.

Nazi storm troopers, known as the SA, took control of the beer hall in what became known as the Beer Hall Putsch, or revolution. Meanwhile Röhm was marching with other troops to take over government offices in Munich. Along with Röhm, marched Heinrich Himmler carrying a flag at the front of the troops. When they reached the War Office Building, however, they were unable to enter it. Instead Röhm and Himmler found themselves surrounded by Bavarian police. Meanwhile, Hitler led his followers from the Beer Hall to rescue Röhm and his supporters. As Hitler approached the War Office Building, he encountered the police. Shots rang out and some of Hitler's men were wounded. Hitler, however, was unhurt. Meanwhile, Röhm's men were forced to surrender. Röhm and Hitler were later sent to prison. The Nazi party was banned from politics. Himmler was more fortunate. Since he was not yet a leader of the Nazis, the government permitted him to go home.

Politics and Elections

Although the Nazis had been largely disbanded, Himmler continued to be involved in politics. He met with Röhm in prison and decided to carry on Röhm's work. Himmler rode his motorbike throughout northern Bavaria, traveling to political meetings. During 1924, Himmler delivered speeches in an effort to get right wing candidates elected to the Reichstag, or German parliament. He also wrote articles presenting Nazi ideas to the German voters. Meanwhile, Himmler had cut himself off from many old friends, who regarded him as a "fanatic."[1] Himmler continued to live at home with his parents, who did not agree with his political views. About this time, Himmler read a pamphlet that described the life of Adolf Hitler and contained some of Hitler's speeches. Himmler also continued reading books that emphasized the importance of racial purity. Like Hitler, Himmler's ideal person was a Nordic German, an Aryan. This was a blond, blue-eyed, tall German, with a long, narrow face. Ironically, it was someone who looked quite different from either Himmler or Hitler. At the same time, Himmler's hatred for the Jews continued to grow. He was convinced that the Jews were involved in a broad effort to take over European governments.[2]

By 1924, few people seemed to agree with Himmler's views or support right-wing radical groups. The German economy was improving, and a majority of Germans wanted to enjoy prosperity. They were not interested in overthrowing the Weimar government. Nevertheless, Himmler continued to work for political groups allied with the Nazis. He also succeeded in finding a new job. Himmler was offered a position by Gregor Strasser, a right-wing leader and a member of the Nazi party. (Although the Nazi party had been banned, it continued to operate.) Strasser was Gauleiter, leader, for Lower Bavaria. He needed someone to handle secretarial duties, keep track of his heavy speaking schedule, and answer letters for him. Himmler was well organized and meticulous at details, as he had proven by his regular diary entries. In July 1924, he became Strasser's deputy.

Rising in the Party

Late in 1924, Hitler was released from prison. During the months he spent behind bars, Hitler had dictated much of *Mein Kampf*, meaning "my struggle." In this book, he set down his strongest views, especially his anti-Semitism. As Hitler wrote:

> Was there any form of filth . . . particularly in cultural
> life, without at least one Jew involved in it? . . . If . . . the
> Jew is victorious over the other peoples of the world,
> his crown will be the funeral wreath of humanity. . . .
> Hence today I believe that I am acting in accordance
> with the will of the Almighty Creator: by defending
> myself against the Jew, I am fighting for the work of
> the Lord.[3]

By early 1925, Hitler had strengthened the Nazi party.
Later that year, Hitler established a special elite group called
the Schutzstaffel (SS), who were to serve as his special
bodyguard. They wore brown shirts, black pants, black ties, a
silver badge in the shape of a skull, as well as a red armband
with the Nazi swastika. Himmler joined the SS in 1925,
becoming head of the unit stationed in Lower Bavaria. His SS
number was 168. The following year, Strasser was named
propaganda minister for the Nazi party, and Himmler served
as his assistant. Himmler relied on members of the SS to
protect Nazi speakers who were sent out to address political
gatherings. Through his work with the SS, Himmler gained a
reputation with the Nazi leaders for efficiency and attention
to detail. In 1927, Himmler was named Deputy Reichsführer,
or leader, of the SS.

In this position, Himmler began to establish the powerful
role that the SS would play in Nazi Germany during the 1930s
and 1940s. In his first order to SS leaders, Himmler stressed
that they should gather intelligence on any "opponents" of
the Nazis, especially any "activity" by "outstanding Jewish
leaders known with certainty to the SS. . . ."[4] As Heinrich
Himmler's biographer Peter Padfield has written: ". . . the
SS was to be at once a secret police and a warrior elite, an
instrument of internal conformity and a breeding ground

for the purification of the race, the hammer of Jews . . . communism and democracy. . . ."[5]

In 1929, Himmler was named by Hitler as head, or Reichsführer, of the SS. At this point, the SS was still a small force. There were only three hundred members of this elite bodyguard for Hitler. Nevertheless, Himmler was intent on turning it into an outstanding organization. Reichsführer Himmler insisted that all SS members must be Aryan. They were also required to marry Aryan women. In fact, each member of the SS was expected to obtain permission or consent from Himmler before getting married. In this way, the SS members could produce Aryan offspring and increase what they saw as the purity of the German race.

Himmler himself had already married a woman who had Aryan characteristics. During the winter of 1926, he had met Margaret—nicknamed Marga—Concerzowo at a hotel in Berchtesgaden, Germany. Eight years older than Himmler, she had blond hair and blue eyes. Margaret had been trained as a nurse and ran a health clinic in Berlin. They were married in 1927. With financial help from Marga, Himmler bought a small farm near Munich, and the couple began raising chickens. In 1929, Marga gave birth to a daughter named Gudrun—nicknamed Puppi—who was the couple's only natural child. Later, they adopted a little boy.

A Nazi Leader

By this time, Himmler had become a recognized leader of the Nazi party. The Nazis carried on torchlight parades. They marched through the streets under their banners, and sang songs that expressed their philosophy. As one of them began:

> Arise Hitler folk, close the ranks
> We're ready for the final racial struggle
> We want to consecrate the flag with blood

As a sign of a new age

Our black swastika shimmers on
a red ground in a white field

. . . We are the true socialists

We don't want reactionaries

We hate the Jews and Marxists [communists].[6]

Nevertheless, the party was still small with only a few seats in the German Reichstag (parliament). However, its position suddenly began to change in 1929. In Germany, the economy had started to decline. Meanwhile, a serious crash occurred on the New York Stock Exchange in October. Gradually the entire world economy fell into a serious depression. Three million people were unemployed in Germany. In the midst of this terrible economic downturn, Germany was still committed to pay reparations to the Allies for another fifty-nine years.

The positions taken by Hitler and the Nazis now seemed more attractive to German voters. In elections held during 1930, the Nazis suddenly became the second largest party in the Reichstag. One of the 107 seats they occupied in the Reichstag was held by Heinrich Himmler. In the Reichstag, Himmler dedicated himself to bringing Hitler and the Nazi party to power. As Himmler told Nazi official Otto Strasser, he was totally committed to Hitler: "For him I could do anything. Believe me, if Hitler were to say I should shoot my mother, I would do it and be proud of his confidence."[7] During 1930, some elements of the Nazi party disagreed with

Heinrich and Marga Himmler and their daughter Gudrun pose outside their home in Germany.

Hitler's leadership and staged a revolt against him. With the help of the SS, Hitler put down the revolt.

Historian Bradley Smith has speculated that Himmler's devotion to Hitler and the Nazi party helped to define him as a person. As a young man he had floundered around, trying to join the army and participate in combat during World War I. Then Himmler had gone to agricultural school, worked on a farm, and briefly been employed by a fertilizer company. Throughout this period, he had been closely tied to his parents and even dominated by his father. After all, Heinrich had pursued the hobbies recommended by his father and kept a diary because his father had required it. By joining the Nazi party, Himmler broke away from his father. He simply traded his father for Hitler and Nazism. As Smith put it:

> . . . Heinrich Himmler was not an adult convert to Nazism; it was through his commitment to the party and its ideology that he became an adult. It was his role as a professional party worker which allowed him to overcome his problems of identity and become a man. An adult Heinrich Himmler separate from the party and its ideology never existed. Himmler was Nazism.[8]

Reichsführer-SS Himmler

As the Nazi party increased its power in Germany, there was opposition among some of its supporters to Hitler's leadership. Part of Himmler's responsibility as head of the SS was to monitor opponents to the Nazi party and expose them before they could undermine Hitler's leadership. A revolt occurred in 1931, but with the help of the SS its leaders were stopped. Hitler knew about the revolt in advance and used the SS to destroy it. As a result, Hitler praised the SS and coined the phrase: "SS man, your honor signifies loyalty." Afterward, this new phrase was printed on all SS belt buckles. Loyalty to the Führer, Adolf Hitler, became the watchword of every member of the SS.[9]

In 1931, Himmler established a new secret service. He appointed a former navy lieutenant named Reinhard Heydrich to direct it. The secret service, or security service, was known as the SD, Sicherheitsdienst. Himmler put it in charge of rooting out political enemies of the Nazis. Heydrich started hiring detectives, some of whom had served in the Weimar police, to become members of the SD. They began setting up extensive files on people who might undermine Hitler's leadership. Some of these people were members of the SA. By 1931, the SA had grown to one hundred thousand strong, under the command of Ernst Röhm. Many of them thought nothing of bashing an opponent's head or setting fire to his home or business if he tried to stand in the way of the Nazis. However, the SA could not always be depended on to follow Hitler's leadership. They wanted more power in the Nazi party, even if it meant defying the orders of Adolf Hitler. Therefore, they had to be watched closely by the SS and the SD. In addition, the SD kept detailed records on leading democratic politicians in the Weimar Republic, as well as communists and Jews.

By mid 1932, the SS had grown to more than forty thousand members.[10] Part of their job was to seek out suspected Communists and kill them. The streets of German cities, like Hamburg, became the scene of violent conflicts. Heydrich sent in SS members to stage large marches. These were designed to provoke the Communists. Firing broke out between the SS and the Communists, in which both SS members and Communists lost their lives. By using these tactics, the Nazis hoped to create political unrest throughout Germany. Voters, they hoped, would then turn to Hitler and

Reinhard Heydrich

Born in 1904, Reinhard Heydrich was the son of a musician and opera singer, named Bruno Heydrich. Bruno's father had died when he was a boy, and his mother had married a man named Gustav Suss. Some people believed that Suss was Jewish, although he was not. As a result, Reinhard Heydrich grew up with some of his friends believing that his grandmother had married a Jew. They also referred to his father as a Jew. To prove that his father was not a Jew, Reinhard became strongly anti-Semitic. He shared this trait with Heinrich Himmler. In addition, Heydrich looked like an outstanding example of the Nordic German, with blond hair and blue eyes.

In 1922, Heydrich had entered the navy and served as an intelligence officer. He had also given his support to right wing military groups and fought against the Communists in Halle, where they had tried to take over the government. Thus his background was similar to Himmler's. In 1931, Heydrich was forced to leave the navy. There are conflicting reports about the reason. It may have been because of his involvement with a woman or because he was a member of the Nazi party. Through a friend, he was introduced to Himmler. Himmler was very impressed with Heydrich, who eventually became his second-in-command.

the Nazis to restore order. By July, the Nazis had become the largest party in the Reichstag, or German Parliament. They had 230 seats.

Early in 1933, the elderly German president, General Paul von Hindenburg—a hero of World War I—reluctantly called on Adolf Hitler to become chancellor of Germany. Hitler received the backing of prominent industrialists and bankers, who believed that the Nazis could improve the German economy and rescue it from the Depression. The SS and SA marched in a giant parade in Berlin. It was observed by a German Jew, Bella Fromm. "In the flickering light of a sea of torches they paraded," she later wrote. "An endless sea of brown. An ominous night. A night of deadly menace, a nightmare in the living reality of 20,000 blazing torches."[11]

The Nazis were about to assume complete power over the German state, with the approval of many powerful interest groups. Among the new leaders of the Nazi government was Reichsführer-SS Heinrich Himmler.

4

Chief of the German Police

On the evening of February 27, 1933, a spectacular fire lit up the sky over Berlin. The German Reichstag was being engulfed in flames. At the scene of the fire, police caught a young pro-Communist and charged him with the crime. Across Germany, the Nazis accused the Communists of attempting to take over the government. Hitler called for new laws giving him more power and eliminating freedom of speech in Germany. In the elections held soon afterward, the Nazis increased their support among the German people. They received 44 percent of the vote, still not a majority. However, the vote was large enough for the Nazis to have a majority of seats in the Reichstag.

As the Nazis consolidated their control, the president of the Reichstag, Hermann Göring, built a power base for himself in Prussia. This was the location of the German capital, Berlin. Göring, a close ally of Hitler, took over the Secret State Police, or Geheime Staatspolizei, which was called the Gestapo. Its headquarters was established at 8 Prinz-Albrecht Strasse—a location that would become infamous throughout Europe. In charge of the Gestapo, Göring placed a young government official named Rudolf Diels, who was loyal to the Nazis.

Meanwhile, Heinrich Himmler stayed close to home in Munich where he set up his own base of power. With the help of his friend Ernst Röhm, who ran the powerful SA, Himmler became Police President of Bavaria. Heydrich was selected to run the local political police. Rapidly, the Nazis began rounding up anyone who seemed to pose a threat to their new regime. These included Communists as well as Jews. The political prisoners were jailed at a new concentration camp that Himmler had ordered opened on March 22. It was located in an old arms factory in a town named Dachau, outside of Munich. To run the camp at Dachau, Himmler selected a loyal member of the SS named Theodor Eicke.

Himmler wrote a news article to describe Dachau.

> . . . the first concentration camp is to be opened in Dachau with an accommodation for 5000 persons. All Communists and—where necessary . . . [politicians] who endanger state security are to be concentrated here. . . . Police Chief Himmler further assured that protective custody is only to be enforced as long as necessary. The widespread rumors regarding the treatment of prisoners are shown to be inaccurate. . . .[1]

By May 1933, there were already twelve hundred prisoners at Dachau—Communists as well as Jews. Regardless of what the article said, the stories about the treatment of political prisoners were more than "rumors." Germans brought to Dachau were brutally treated by the SS guards. They were often starved, beaten repeatedly with heavy whips, and even

Deutsche!
Wehrt Euch!
Kauft nicht bei Juden!

killed during their torture by the SS. Others were shot, supposedly while trying to escape the camp.

Some prisoners were released after their experience at Dachau. They served as a warning to others in German society of the punishment that might await them if they defied the Nazis. Himmler used this approach to instill terror throughout Bavaria. Later he would expand the terror across Germany and the rest of Europe. In fact, members of the SS, who later became the commandants of other concentration camps, received their early training at Dachau.

Himmler Increases His Power

In early 1933, from his political base in Bavaria, Himmler gradually expanded his power. At this time, Hitler had already become chancellor, but General von Hindenburg was still president of Germany. While the Nazis were the strongest party in the country, they had not yet taken over total control of the state.

Historian George Browder explained that in Bavaria, Himmler built a triangular power structure. It consisted of three parts, like the points of a triangle. These three parts were the SS, the political police in Bavaria, and the concentration camps, which began to grow in number.[2] These instruments enabled him to spy on suspected enemies of the Nazi state. Then he could order the arrest of those considered to be enemies of the Nazis. Finally, they could be imprisoned in concentration camps and brutally punished. Himmler

An SS guard stands next to a German store after the boycott against Jewish businesses was enacted. The sign in German reads: "Germans! Defend yourselves! Do not buy from Jews!"

would eventually use the same approach across the country. It would create terror among those who opposed the Nazis.

From Bavaria, Himmler planned to increase his power to other parts of Germany. For example, some of his SS officers began to work closely with the Gestapo in Prussia. Himmler befriended local political leaders in Hamburg and even appointed one of them an honorary general in the SS. A similar event occurred in the German city of Lubeck. According to Browder, Himmler also suggested to local officials that his activities were completely supported by Adolf Hitler. Historians are not certain whether Hitler had actually given his complete support to Himmler in 1933, or whether this only happened later. Nevertheless, Himmler acted as if he had Hitler's total backing.[3] By the end of the year, he had expanded his control of the police throughout Germany, except the Gestapo in Berlin, which was still led by Göring.

Strengthening the SS

As his power grew, Himmler built up the SS as the elite corps of Nazi Germany. According to biographer Peter Padfield, Himmler played the role of a stern father to his men, who genuinely seemed to love him. He acted as their "father-counselor" when they needed one.[4] However, if they disobeyed the rules of the SS, Himmler would punish them. One officer felt Himmler's strict observance of the rules when he mentioned some confidential information to a girl. The officer was immediately demoted. Another man, Himmler's chauffeur, was thrown into prison for being in a car accident.[5]

As Himmler's position in Germany improved, so did his lifestyle. He had a chauffeur-driven car. He had also purchased a magnificent new home for his small family,

Karl Wolff

In expanding his power, Himmler was assisted by Karl Wolff. Himmler had appointed him as his adjutant-assistant. Born in 1900, Wolff looked the true Aryan—tall, blue eyed, with blond hair. Wolff had grown up in Munich, where his parents sent him to an exclusive elementary school. He had received a medal for bravery during World War I. In the 1920s, Wolff opened a successful advertising firm. During the economic depression of the early 1930s, however, Wolff's firm had run into financial problems. Finally, in 1931 after leaving the advertising business, Wolff joined the SS and attended officer training school. Wolf's efficiency as well as his appearance as a German Aryan appealed to Himmler. He later became chief of Himmler's personal staff.

Marga, Puppi, and their adopted son, overlooking a lake near Munich, Germany.

Meanwhile, within the ranks of the SS, Himmler was trying to build a group of men similar to the knights of medieval Europe. These soldiers lived by a code of chivalry. The code included honesty, defending the weak, destroying evil, and protecting the Christian Church. Unfortunately, this code did not reflect the behavior of the SS in rounding up political prisoners. Nevertheless, Himmler imagined that the SS was a band of chivalrous knights. He established a special headquarters for them at a medieval castle in Germany, called Wewelsburg. Here the knights of the SS gathered to eat elaborate dinners, talk about the future of Germany, and discuss their plans. It seemed to make little difference to Himmler that instead of being brave knights, they were engaged in a brutal effort to destroy their enemies and control Germany. As he told them, "Never forget, we are a knightly Order, from which one cannot withdraw, to which one is recruited by blood and within which one remains with body and soul so long as one lives on this earth."[6]

SS officers were rigorously trained at schools such as Bad Tölz, located in the Bavarian Alps. They were expected to excel at noble, manly sports, like boxing, fencing, or horseback riding. They were also taught military skills, such as map reading, marksmanship, mountain climbing, how to handle machine guns in combat, and how to lead attacks against enemy positions. As part of their training, they were expected to swear an oath to Hitler. First they were asked, "Why do we believe in Germany and the Führer?" Their answer in the oath was: "Because we believe in God, we believe in Germany which He created in His world and in the Führer, Adolf Hitler, whom He has sent us." The oath was

Officer Ranks in the SS

SS-Oberstgruppenführer	Colonel-General
SS-Obergruppenführer	General
SS-Standartenführer	Colonel
SS-Sturmbannführer	Major
SS-Hauptsturmführer	Captain
SS-Obersturmführer	First Lieutenant

taken during a special midnight ceremony. As one new SS member put it, reciting the oath brought tears to "my eyes, when, by the light of torches, thousands of voices repeated the oath in chorus. It was like a prayer."[7]

Indeed, Himmler wanted the loyalty of the SS to Hitler and the Third Reich to replace religion, according to historian Michael Burleigh. The Catholic Church was founded on a set of values that emphasized love of others and individual sacrifice for their needs. In contrast, SS men were supposed to be tough and ruthless. These values were directly opposed to Christianity. It was obviously a contradiction to Himmler's view that the SS should be like the chivalrous knights of the past, who had been Christians. The Nazis were especially eager to remove Jesus Christ from his central role in Christian religion. Christianity was related to Judaism. Christ, who had founded Christianity, was a Jew. But the Nazis tried to pretend that he was a member of the Nordic race. Instead of recognizing a church or God or Jesus Christ as a higher authority, the SS was expected to recognize Hitler

49

as their leader. The SS attacked Catholic priests and other members of the Christian clergy. However, Himmler emphasized that vices such as alcoholism, which was condemned by the Christian churches, must also be avoided by all SS members.[8]

The Night of the Long Knives

While Himmler was expanding the power of the SS, his old friend Ernst Röhm was encountering problems. Röhm headed the SA, which had grown to over 4 million strong. Many of the military leaders and industrialists who had backed Hitler wanted him to exert control over the SA. Its members roamed the streets, threatening store owners if they did not pay them protection money—that is, bribes. Many Germans feared that they might be attacked by the SA unless they gave it their complete support. Hitler also feared that Röhm and the SA threatened the position of the professional German army. Hitler needed the support of the army to remain in power.

Hitler recognized that he must reduce the role of the SA, which he feared might eventually undermine his own position. In order to accomplish this task, he needed the help of the SS and Himmler. This was the only internal police force powerful enough to attack the SA and remove its leaders, such as Röhm. Hitler decided to strengthen Himmler's position for the confrontation with the SA that lay ahead. During spring 1934, Himmler was given control of the Gestapo in Berlin. Himmler, Heydrich, and Wolff moved to No. 8 Prinz-Albrecht Strasse to establish their new headquarters. The SD was also expanding. They were better educated than many members of the Nazi party. Over 40 percent of SD members had more than a basic secondary (high school) education.[9]

Meanwhile, the planning began for an attack on Röhm and other leaders whom Hitler feared might not be entirely loyal to him. These included another old friend and supporter of Himmler's, Gregor Strasser. Heydrich, as leader of the SD, collected evidence against Röhm and Strasser. This evidence supposedly linked them to a planned overthrow of Hitler and his government. The attack on Röhm and the other leaders began on the night of June 30, 1934. The SS broke into their homes and shot some of them. Others were dragged off to prison and executed there. These included Röhm and Strasser. As many as 200 to 250 top Nazis were killed during the attack, which was called the Night of the Long Knives.[10]

Himmler had played a key role during the Night of the Long Knives. He had proven his loyalty to Hitler, who did not forget him for it. Hitler enlarged his power and promoted his loyal assistants, Heydrich and Wolff. As far as Himmler was concerned, supporting Hitler was more important than acting "against his first chief, Gregor Strasser, and his early friend and mentor . . . Röhm. . . ."[11] Following the death of Strasser, the SS—subordinate to the SA in the past—became independent. Himmler reported directly to Hitler. This gave Himmler far more power and influence.

A Leader of the State

By the middle of 1934, Adolf Hitler had established himself as the Führer of Germany. President von Hindenburg was dead. The Nazis had also taken control of the press and eliminated all other political parties. From Himmler's viewpoint, Hitler and the Nazi leadership were bringing a great new era to Germany. As Himmler told his SS officers: "He [Hitler] has set us the goal for our generation to be a new beginning. . . . And already he has in fact established the beginning of a new thousands of years of German future and German history."[12]

Himmler already played an important role in the Third Reich. This was the name of the new thousand-year empire that Hitler was beginning to establish during his rule in Germany. In January 1935, Himmler toured the SS training camps, accompanied by his wife, Marga. In his speeches, he constantly emphasized the importance of maintaining the racial purity of the SS officers and carrying on the battle against the Jews who threatened the Nazi state.

Indeed, the battle had already begun. In 1935, one German woman, known only as Christa M., recalled seeing a group of SA soldiers,

> with their boots and caps and armbands—they always wore the swastika armband. In the center there was a man in a long black robe and a long beard. They had put a big drum around his neck. They were pushing him and shoving him. And he had to beat the drum, and he had to say to the drum, "I'm a filthy Jew. I'm a filthy Jew." And they shoved him and tried to even trip him. Every time he staggered or fell, they kicked him again. It was just horrible, horrible, horrible, horrible.[13]

In September 1935, Hitler gave an address at a large rally of the Nazi party held in Nuremberg, Germany. Huge Nazi flags and banners waved above the heads of thousands of loyal supporters of Germany's leader. During his speech, Hitler discussed the so-called Nuremberg Laws. According to these regulations, Jews were now forced to accept an inferior position in the German Reich. The laws stated that a "Jew cannot be a citizen of the Reich. He cannot exercise the right to vote; he cannot hold public office." The Nuremberg Laws also defined a Jew as "an individual who is descended from at least three grandparents who were, racially, full Jews [and] also an individual who is descended from two full-Jewish grandparents" under certain conditions. These included being a member of the Jewish religion and being married to a Jew.[14]

As a result of the Nuremberg Laws, Jews were prevented from marrying Aryan Germans. In addition, no Jews could display the German flag on their homes. Jews were defined as anyone with at least two Jewish grandparents. Even half-Jews were prohibited from marrying Aryans. Such a marriage might produce offspring that would undermine the racial purity of Aryan Germans. As a result of the new laws, Jews could be singled out to be persecuted throughout Germany.

Himmler fully supported the Nuremberg Laws. He was a strong believer in achieving racial purity among the German people. In order to expand this racial purity, Himmler started the Lebensborn—Fountain of Life—in December 1935. This organization was designed to help Nordic mothers who had been involved in relationships with SS men. Lebensborn set up homes for these women and their babies. The women had an opportunity to raise their children, who were considered racially pure members of the German master race. If the women were unable to raise them, the Lebensborn arranged for families to adopt them and teach the children to become loyal Nazis. Many Lebensborn maternity homes were set up across Germany.

As a way of spreading the values of the SS, Himmler began a newspaper called *The Black Corps*. The "black corps" was a nickname for the SS, who dressed almost entirely in black. As he told his officers:

> . . . we are joined in battle with the oldest enemy our *Volk* [our people] has had for centuries—with Jews. . . . We did not seek this battle. It is there, it must be there, as it has always been there in history as Germany, after bleeding to death, rose from the ground and regrouped its forces. It is there according to historical law.[15]

The Nazis issued charts showing what were supposed to be the racial characteristics of Jews, such as large hook noses. Though in reality not all Jews looked this way, some suffered persecution because of the Nazi guidelines. One boy, named Frank S., recalled "his mother gently kneading his younger brother's large nose to make it straight and thus protect him from attacks by Nazis." Later Frank went to work for an electrician, a Nazi, who made him do all the extra heavy work because he was a Jew.[16]

Germans who befriended Jews might be dragged in by the Gestapo for questioning. One Jewish woman, Edith P., recalled that all Germans were not necessarily opposed to Jews, but just "passive. Maybe they were scared." Another Jew added that there was a fear of being denounced—turned in to the Gestapo—if somebody tried to help a Jewish person. As one German woman recalled, as a child she was told in school "Jews are dirty. They are root of all evil. Whatever is going to happen to us that's bad, whatever that did happen that's bad, it's all the fault of the Jews. The Jews own all the money. The Jews are all crooks and all Jews are going to cheat you. Never trust them."[17]

By this time, Himmler had woven together an impressive power base. It included the SS, the SD, and the Gestapo. Many Germans feared the Gestapo, which seemed to have agents throughout the country. In addition, there was widespread fear that ordinary citizens were informing the Gestapo of any activity that seemed to threaten the Nazi state. As one German, Victor Klemperer, put it: "No letter,

Himmler (third from left) poses with Adolf Hitler (third from right) and other Nazi leaders in Nuremberg, Germany, on Nazi Party Day in 1935.

no telephone conversation, no word on the street is safe any more. Everyone fears the next person may be an informer."[18]

In addition, Himmler controlled the concentration camps, which were run by the brutal guard units called "Death's Head Formations." Any citizen of Germany who seemed to oppose the Führer, Adolf Hitler, could be investigated by the SD, arrested by the Gestapo, and sent away to a concentration camp, most of them never to return.

Himmler's Expanding Empire

In recognition of Himmler's position in Germany, Hitler promoted him to Chief of the German Police in 1936. In return, Himmler swore his loyalty to the Führer and expected the SS to do the same thing. "Whether our actions run counter to [the law] is of absolutely no consequence to me," Himmler said late in 1936. "In fulfilling my task, I do basically what I can answer for to my conscience in my work for Führer and Volk. . . ."[19]

Meanwhile, Heydrich's responsibilities also expanded. In addition to directing the SD, he also became head of the Security Police, Sicherheitspolizei. This new organization included the Gestapo, as well as the police charged with arresting criminals. Inside the SD, there were specific departments that focused on rounding up certain types of enemies of the Nazi state. These included Jews as well as Communists and Freemasons. The Freemasons were a secret society founded during the eighteenth century. They had lodges—or clubs—throughout Europe. The Nazis regarded any secret society as a threat to their power.

Adolf Eichmann rose quickly through the ranks of the SD. He took his orders from Heydrich and Himmler.

Joining the SD to keep lists of Freemasons was a young Nazi named Adolf Eichmann. His job was to compile lists of Freemasons in countries throughout Europe. The SD was already preparing for the day when Germany might expand again, just as it did in World War I. Then these Freemasons would be arrested and sent to concentration camps. After working for a short time in the Freemason section, Eichmann was transferred to the Jewish section. Here he compiled lists of leading Jews throughout Germany and the rest of Europe. In addition to keeping the names of these Jews, the SD also kept watch on Jewish organizations to find out what types of activities their members were carrying on.

The work of the SD simply reflected the general attitude of the Nazis toward the Jews. After the Nazis came to power, Jews had little by little lost their citizenship in the Nazi state. Many Jewish doctors were prevented from practicing medicine; Jewish lawyers were forbidden from practicing law; and Jews were banned from holding political office. Jewish merchants were regularly forced out of business by being denied credit from German banks, or following visits by Gestapo thugs who arrested them. Signs went up on many German restaurants, swimming pools, and other public places saying "Jews not wanted here." Although many Jews had served in the German army during World War I, the Nazis now prevented them from joining the military.

Jews were being forced to leave Germany, while others who seemed to pose a threat to the state were being rounded up and put into concentration camps. By 1938, Himmler had established new concentration camps in addition to Dachau. The SS established camps at Sachsenhausen outside of Berlin in 1936, Flossenburg in Bavaria in 1938, and at Buchenwald near Weimar.

The construction of Buchenwald, one of the most notorious concentration camps, was begun in July 1937. It was located on top of a fifteen-hundred-foot hill. Prisoners from Sachsenhausen were brought there to construct the camp under the direction of the SS. Jewish prisoners began arriving at Buchenwald in spring 1938.

Construction of Sachsenhausen began during the summer of 1936. The prisoners ordered to build the concentration camp were harshly treated by the SS, and many of them died. Buildings were constructed of wood and bricks to house political opponents, Jews, and other types of prisoners who began arriving at the camp after it was completed.

The camps held a variety of prisoners who were being rounded up by the Gestapo and forced to wear distinctive identification badges. These badges appeared on the left side of their jackets and right side of their pants. Political enemies wore red badges, while homeless people wore black badges. Jews wore yellow badges, while criminals wore green badges. Homosexuals were forced to wear pink badges in the shape of triangles. Prisoners inside the camps were treated brutally by the SS guards. The guards kicked and punched inmates, sexually abused some of them, and tortured them regularly. At one camp, historian Michael Burleigh wrote: "Bored guards . . . periodically chucked 'parachutists' [inmates] off the rim [of rock quarries] by way of entertainment."[20]

In addition to their work inside the German concentration camps, the SS and the SD had enlisted agents to do intelligence work in various countries bordering Germany. They included Czechoslovakia and Poland. These agents carried on surveillance of political leaders. They collected information on important Jews. All of this information was carefully collected and put on note cards. In the future, if the Nazis took over one of these neighboring countries, the Jews and the political leaders could easily be rounded up. Then they would be imprisoned in concentration camps. In addition, the SD trained hit men who were sent in to murder politicians who were hostile to the Third Reich. Their role was to prepare the way for a time when German armies might move against these countries and conquer them.

By 1938, that time had come.

Persecuting Jews on Germany's Borders

On March 14, 1938, Heinrich Himmler entered Vienna, Austria, along with his Führer, Adolf Hitler. Wearing a gray uniform, which was the standard dress for the SS when it was involved in a military campaign, Himmler celebrated the Anschluss—the annexation of Austria. A short time earlier, Nazi troops had poured across the German border, occupying Austria and making it part of the Greater German Reich. Hitler had been born in Austria and spent part of his early life in Vienna, before moving to Munich, Germany. The German leader believed that his birthplace should become part of the new German empire. Himmler was just as firmly convinced that he must carry out Hitler's wishes in Austria—rounding up Jews, Communists, and others who might threaten the Reich, just as he was doing in Germany.

Led by Reinhard Heydrich, the SS immediately began arresting people, loading them aboard trains, and shipping them to Dachau. Others were sent to a new concentration camp, which Himmler opened at Mauthausen along the Danube River. This camp was constructed by prisoners from Dachau. Mauthausen would enable the Nazis to house the large numbers of undesirable people they expected to imprison in Austria. At Mauthausen, Jews and other prisoners were forced to work in a rock quarry. The stone was sold in other parts of the Third Reich for construction projects. Approximately two hundred thousand inmates would be imprisoned at Mauthausen. An estimated one hundred twenty thousand died there from starvation, torture, and overwork. One special type of torture required prisoners to carry a rock weighing one hundred pounds on their shoulders up almost two hundred steps from the rock quarry. It was called "the staircase of death." Those who failed were forced to go back and try again. Some committed suicide by jumping into the quarry, rather than submit to the torture. Many others died while trying to carry the heavy rocks.[1]

Meanwhile, Himmler and Heydrich began to expand the SS in Austria, recruiting men who fit the pure Nordic profile. Himmler needed more SS members to police the newly enlarged German Reich. As Himmler put it, there were several types of people who must be removed from Austrian society. They included:

> professional criminals who have committed a small murder, a small break-in or something of that sort. . . . The second group consists of political prisoners. This is a more evil company. . . . Then comes the third group. It represents the refuse of humanity, the carrion of our social life, bloodsuckers, exploiters—in short, Jews.[2]

Reinhard Heydrich (center) was chief of the Nazi security police. Here, he poses with Himmler (left) and another officer during a visit to Paris, France.

The Nazi takeover of Austria unleashed a firestorm against the Jews. The same thing was already happening in Germany. Jews were forced to give up their jobs. Instead, they were put to work by the Nazi government cleaning streets and sidewalks, often with no more than toothbrushes. In addition to this type of humiliating treatment, Jews were paraded into local parks and forced to eat grass like animals. Other Jews were required to run around without stopping, until some of the elderly died of heart attacks. By the end of 1938, an estimated forty thousand Austrian Jewish families had been forced out of their homes, which were promptly given to Gentiles (non-Jews). Many Jewish merchants were also driven out of their businesses, which were turned over to Gentiles. As an example, one Jewish merchant, Josef Bien, owned a fur business. The business was attacked by Nazis who stole several thousand dollars and a large quantity of furs from Bien's store. Public places, such as movie theaters and restaurants, were closed to Jews. These facilities posted signs that read: "Jews not wanted here."

Turning to Czechoslovakia

No sooner had the Nazis taken control of Austria, than Hitler turned his attention to another neighbor across the German border—Czechoslovakia. Over 3 million Germans lived in the western part of the country, an area called the Sudetenland. Hitler wanted to annex the Sudetenland, making it part of the German Reich, and eventually absorb all of Czechoslovakia. During the spring of 1938, Heydrich was preparing a file of Czechs who had to be removed from the country after the Nazi takeover. He also sent his agents into the Sudetenland. These agents helped organize demonstrations among the Germans and encourage them to demand that they be united with the German Reich.

France and Great Britain had pledged themselves to support Czechoslovakia. However, the British prime minister, Neville Chamberlain, wanted to avoid war with Germany at this time. Therefore, he supported a policy of appeasement—satisfying Hitler's demands for the Sudetenland. Chamberlain flew to Germany for a series of meetings with Hitler during September 1938. Chamberlain listened as the Führer insisted that the Sudetenland should become part of Germany. Finally, at Munich on September 29–30, 1938, Chamberlain, along with French Prime Minister Edouard Daladier, caved in to Hitler's demands.

Chamberlain flew home to England, saying that he had achieved "peace in our time." However, another English political leader, Winston Churchill, saw the situation more clearly. Churchill had served in previous British governments during World War I and the 1920s. In order to avoid war, Churchill said, "we have chosen shame, and we will get war."[3] The Nazis had taken the Sudetenland, but Hitler was not satisfied. Over the next few months, Heydrich directed teams of SS agents into the other parts of Czechoslovakia. They blew up factories and tried to make the sabotage look like the work of Czechs who were opposed to the local government. The SS organized giant street marches demanding an overthrow of the Czech government. Finally, Czech political leaders were forced to resign and hand over the government to Germany. In mid March 1939, Hitler rode into Prague, the capital of Czechoslovakia. Once again, as he had been in Austria, Hitler was accompanied by Himmler.

SS units and the Gestapo set up a network throughout Czechoslovakia. Jews were ordered to wear yellow stars to identify themselves. Renee H. was six years old at the time. "I remember coming home one day and seeing my mother sewing on the star on my coat. And I was aware of the fact that this was a way of singling us out. I remember saying, 'Let's not do this, because then we can't hide.' And she said, 'We have to. This is the decree.'"[4] They had already prepared lists of people to be rounded up and taken to concentration camps. In addition, the SS began to look for new recruits to increase their ranks. In this way, they would have enough officials to carry on their brutal work inside Czechoslovakia.

Kristallnacht

Meanwhile, the treatment of the Jews in Germany had grown much worse. A pogrom—a campaign of organized violence—broke out against the Jews. It was touched off by an incident that had occurred in Paris. The French capital was the home of a young unemployed Polish Jew named Herschel Grynszpan. His family had been living in Germany, but in early October they were driven out by the Nazi authorities. Grynszpan received a note, describing the plight of his parents and sisters. As he later explained: "I acted . . . because of love for my parents and for my people who were subjected unjustly to outrageous treatment . . . It is not, after all, a crime to be Jewish. I am not a dog. I have the right to live. My people have a right to exist on this earth."[5]

On November 7, Grynszpan walked into the German embassy in Paris, met with a diplomat named Ernst vom Rath, and shot him with a gun. Grynszpan was arrested shortly afterward by the French police. On November 9 and 10, across Germany and Austria, violence broke out directed at Jews. Historians are not sure who ordered the violence. It may have been Hitler, himself, or Himmler. No records indicate who made the decision.[6] With the help of SS agents, angry Germans destroyed Jewish stores and burned synagogues. An order from Gestapo headquarters directed that police officials should stand by and let the violence occur. Orders were also given to arrest twenty thousand to thirty thousand Jewish leaders. The pogrom came to be called Kristallnacht, meaning "the night of broken glass," because of the glass windows that were broken in Jewish shops. According to one estimate, seventy-five hundred Jewish businesses were looted. Over 175 synagogues were destroyed, and 91 Jews were killed.[7] The Nazis broke into the homes of Jews and attacked them while their families watched the bloodshed. Jews were stabbed with knives and hit with shovels. One Jew was dragged from his home and stoned to death.

One Jewish girl, Golly D., was sixteen years old at the time of the incident. Her family lived in Bremen, Germany. She remembered a pounding on the door of her house as Nazi troops demanded entry. Her family was told by the Nazis to get dressed; then they were immediately led away to a mess hall. Many other Jews had been brought there, too. The Nazis let them sit for hours,

> until they separated the women from the men and the men were taken away. We didn't know where to, and so was my father and my brother. In the morning, my mother and I and all women were allowed to return home. . . . My father's business was destroyed that night. And of course we had one synagogue in Bremen, which was burned down. The next day, not suspecting anything, I returned to school, the day after the *Kristallnacht.* [I] walked up the steps trying to get to my classroom, and my homeroom teacher, Mr. Koch, came down the steps, by coincidence, and approached me and said to me really with sad eyes, "Miss Golly, I'm awfully sorry, but Jews are no longer to attend school." So I had no choice but to turn back. And I walked home with my head down, and I realized that my plans for the future had been shattered.[8]

Kristallnacht had been aimed at all Jews who got in the way of the Nazis. Many Jews, possibly including Golly's father and brother, were taken to concentration camps. One Jew imprisoned at Sachsenhausen remembers the camp commandant saying to all the prisoners:

> You are here to atone for the cowardly assassination committed by your Polish racial comrade Grusnspan [Grynszpan]. You must remain here as hostages so that world Jewry carries out no more murders. . . . Every SS order is to be obeyed. If they wish, the SS has the right to shoot you. . . . There is therefore no point in trying to escape. The barbed wire around the camp is electrified. Whoever touches it will die instantly.[9]

Within Germany, Hitler and other Nazi leaders believed that the Jews had brought the violence on themselves. Hitler blamed them for creating conflict between Germany, France, and Great Britain. As he told a group of German political leaders at the Reichstag in January 1939:

> In my life I have often been a prophet. . . . Today I want to be a prophet again: If international . . . Jewry inside and outside Europe again succeeds in precipitating the nations into a world war, the result will not be the Bolshevisation of the earth, and with it the victory of Jewry, but the annihilation of the Jewish race in Europe.[10]

As more and more Jews were removed from German society, Himmler ordered the construction of another concentration camp to imprison them. Fifty miles north of Berlin, Ravensbrück concentration camp was built as a facility for females who were being held by the SS. Construction began at the end of 1938. Prisoners were brought from Sachsenhausen to build the camp, which included fourteen barracks and a kitchen. The first prisoners arrived in May 1939.

Himmler and Poland

Following his success in Austria and Czechoslovakia, Hitler turned his attention to Poland. Early in 1939, he had demanded that the Polish government turn over the port city of Danzig (Gdansk) to Germany. Hitler made it clear that if the Poles refused, he was prepared to take control of it. Although Hitler may have thought that the Poles would back down, just as the Austrians and Czechs had done, he was mistaken. As historian Norman Davies wrote:

> Unfortunately, neither Hitler nor those who advised him knew much about Poland's mettle. . . . They did not know that Polish colonels . . . were not going to bow and scrape to an ex-Austrian corporal (Hitler's rank during World War I). Their instinct was to fight, and to go down fighting. Every single Polish official who had to deal with Nazi . . . threats in 1939 had been reared on the . . . moral testament: "To be defeated, but not to surrender, that is victory."[11]

While Hitler confronted Poland, Himmler had been stricken with an unknown illness. Biographer Peter Padfield explained that he was suffering from painful stomach cramps that literally knocked him out. These may have been brought on, according to Padfield, by his increased duties as the German empire expanded. Himmler was a very hard worker, who put in long hours at his desk, overseeing every detail of his office. Although the stomach problems may have resulted from overwork, Himmler feared that he had cancer. His father had recently died of stomach cancer. Himmler agreed to have a doctor examine him. However, he did not want the information to get out that he might be ill. This would not have seemed appropriate for the image that Himmler tried to present—a strong, tough Aryan.[12]

While Himmler grappled with his stomach problems, the situation in eastern Europe grew worse. The Poles ignored the Nazi demands. They also received a guarantee from Great Britain to stand by Poland in case of war. Meanwhile, Hitler prepared a battle plan for the invasion of Poland, called Case White. In August 1939, German diplomats concluded an agreement with the Soviet Union to cooperate in an attack on the Poles. Therefore, Poland found itself trapped between Germany and the Soviets. On August 24, the German armies were ready to roll across the Polish border. But, at the last minute, Hitler waited. According to historian Norman Davies, he was "curious to see if a second Munich was possible."[13] But neither the Poles nor their allies were prepared to back down.

In order to create a reason for the invasion, Heydrich was ordered to stage an incident on the German/Polish border. On the night of August 31, SS men dressed as Poles attacked a German radio station on the international border. The SS brought an innocent young Pole to the station and shot him there, to make the attack look more authentic. Meanwhile, inmates from a concentration camp were brought to the scene, wearing Polish uniforms. They were ordered to attack the station, and then were shot by the SS.[14]

On September 1, 1939, the Nazis attacked Poland. Traveling with the army were military units of the SS. These Einsatzgruppen, as they were called, were formed into four-hundred- to six-hundred-man units. These units were attached to each of the five Nazi armies that had attacked Poland. In charge of the Einsatzgruppen was the Reich Security Head Office—RSHA—which had been newly established by Himmler to direct SS activities in Poland. The RSHA was commanded by Heydrich.

Lucy Krugieski

Jakub Krugieski was mayor of Poznan, a city in Poland. When the SS entered his city, Krugieski and his wife, Magadalena, were among the people who were taken from their homes. Fortunately, their eighteen-year-old daughter Lucy (born in 1921 in Poznan), had gone to the stable to feed her horse so she was not captured by the SS. "As I returned from the stable," she said, "I saw in the rear garden about fifty men in uniforms, some wearing helmets, others in soft caps, carrying machine guns. They had their backs to me." They were about to shoot Lucy's parents and other Poles lined up against the wall. Lucy's father saw her and yelled, "Run!" With that, shots rang out and the Krugieskis were killed. But Lucy escaped to the woods. Later, she was caught and sent to Hamburg, a city in Germany. There she was forced to work as a maid.[15]

The SS in Poland

As the SS entered cities and villages across Poland, they came armed with lists of people to be eliminated. These included political leaders, Jews, Communists, and Catholics. In one area, the SS murdered 214 Catholic priests. Many more Jews were rounded up, and some of them were machine-gunned in their own synagogues.

The SS carried on its work in Poland very efficiently. Its job was to eliminate the leaders of Polish society who might lead the resistance against the Nazis. According to one estimate, the SS killed two hundred Poles per day. By the end of September, Heydrich reported: "Of the Polish upper classes in the occupied territories only a maximum of three percent is still present."[16] On October 5, 1939, Himmler accompanied Hitler on his entrance into Warsaw, the capital of Poland. The Nazis had taken control of part of the country, while the Soviets had invaded from the east and taken the rest.

Some of the German military were opposed to the violent work carried on by the SS in Poland. They believed that the Germans had no right to murder Jews, Bolsheviks, or Polish political leaders. Nevertheless, Himmler continued his efforts to destroy the enemies of the Reich. At one university in Kraków, Poland, for example, the SS rounded up every professor and took them to Sachsenhausen concentration camp. Approximately seventeen hundred Catholic priests were transported to Dachau, where many died. Leading Polish intellectuals were shot. As Hitler later said: "There can only be one master for the Poles, and that should be the German; there cannot, and should not, be two masters side by side, and therefore all representatives of the Polish intelligentsia are to be killed. That sounds harsh, but it is only the law of life." Himmler agreed with the Führer.[17]

Jews immediately felt the presence of the Nazis following the invasion. One young Polish Jew recalled that the Jewish population of his town were not permitted to go to their synagogue. In fact, it was burned and all the sacred prayer books were destroyed.[18]

Once the battle for Poland had ended, Hitler gave Himmler a new title, Reichskommissar for the Consolidation of German Nationhood. This meant that, among other things, Himmler would have complete responsibility for the ethnic cleansing of Poland. Jews and non-Jewish Polish people would be killed or moved out of vast areas of the country. In their place, Germans would be moved in to operate farms and run businesses owned by the Jews. One of the reasons that Hitler had invaded Poland was to provide additional living space for pure Aryan Germans. Hitler called this Lebensraum—living space for the expanding German population. Both Hitler and Himmler believed strongly that their role as leaders of Germany was to cleanse areas like Poland of inferior races, such as the Jews, and replace them with members of the German master race. As Himmler drove along the roadways in the east, he would stop, get out of the car, and pick up a handful of soil from beside the road. This soil, he hoped, would soon be cultivated by German farmers.[19] The Poles would be reduced to slaves who would be expected to work on the German farms and do whatever they were told.

Himmler imagined new German villages being constructed in Poland. Plans were developed and models of the villages were created. Himmler also held competitions among German architects to determine who would design these villages. These villages, however, were not constructed. The money was needed to pursue the war. Nevertheless, Himmler succeeded in moving almost five hundred thousand new settlers into Poland.

During the fall and winter of 1939–1940, Jews were forcibly evicted from their homes to make way for new German settlers. An estimated 1.5 million Jews and others in Poland were targeted for removal. Some were loaded into railroad cars and taken to cities. There they were forced to find homes in over-crowded ghettos—separate areas for Jews. In Warsaw, Jews were required to move into a ghetto and construct a wall around it. This would separate them from the rest of the city and make the task of keeping them under control easier for the SS. The wall was eleven feet high with broken glass cemented into it at the top. Gates in and out of the ghetto were closed off in 1940. Jews could no longer leave to work or find food. The Nazis allowed a small amount of food to be transported inside the Warsaw ghetto. But it was barely enough to keep people alive. By early 1941, 445,000 Jews were living in the Warsaw ghetto. They had been transported there from other parts of Poland.

Other ghettos were constructed in cities across Poland, including Kraków, Grodno, Lublin, and Lodz. Nina Kaleska recalled that her family was forced to move into the ghetto at Grodno. "And that I remember very distinctly and with great pain," she said. ". . . The Germans would come in and . . . remove the most beautiful china and just throw it against a wall to break it, for fun, and started to taunt and tease."[20]

In Lublin, according to a Jewish journalist, conditions were so bad that:

> men die like flies in the thoroughfares, their bodies strewn on the roadway like old cinders. . . . At night everything is pitch black. . . . Chairs, wardrobes, even beds have long since been chopped up for firewood. . . .

> The whole city is girt with barbed-wire fences, and the
> Nazis allow no traffic to pass through it.[21]

Approximately one hundred fifty thousand Jews were forcibly moved to the Lodz ghetto in 1940. Over the next two years, another fifty thousand Jews would be moved to Lodz from Germany, Czechoslovakia, and Austria.

Many other Jews were taken to the eastern sections of Poland. This area was known as the General Government. It was a separate area, ruled by the Nazis, and not considered part of Germany. Here they were dumped out with no homes in which to live. Many died during this terrible ordeal, freezing to death in the winter cold. Some were shot by the SS. It was a difficult job, Himmler told his SS officers. "In many cases it is much easier to go into battle with a company of infantry than it is to suppress an obstructive population of low cultural level, or to carry out executions, or to haul people away, or to evict crying and hysterical women."[22] Nevertheless, the SS carried out its job ruthlessly and efficiently.

Meanwhile, Himmler was establishing new Lebensborn homes throughout Poland. Children who looked Aryan in appearance were taken from their parents and moved to the homes. Then they were adopted by SS couples who were supposed to raise them to become loyal Nazis. Polish girls who looked Aryan were taken to Germany and forced to work as maids for Nazi families. Here they were also supposed to learn to be Germans. Eventually, Himmler expected them to produce children and increase the Aryan race. Himmler called this project Operation Nursemaid.

These programs were part of Himmler's effort to increase the racial purity of eastern Europe—eliminate Jews and others who seemed racially inferior and replace them with Aryans. During the early months of 1940, some Jews were taken from Warsaw and other locations and shot by SS execution squads. Himmler also ordered the construction of a new concentration camp in Poland. Called Auschwitz, construction began in mid 1940. Himmler placed the camp under the command of Rudolf Höss. Polish prisoners began to be sent to the camp in June.

The prisoners lived in cold, damp blocks of prison cells. These were located in brick buildings, heavily guarded by the SS. Around the entire camp was an electrified fence that carried 6,000 volts of electricity. Perhaps the most terrible area of the camp was Block 11. According to one SS guard:

> Breathing was almost impossible. Many prisoners were doomed to spend there, naturally without a single ray of light, terrible hours or even weeks. It was out of the question to sit down. The prisoners cowered in the darkness. When the cold in the winter was severe, it was impossible to get warm moving about.

Many prisoners died in these cells. Each cell held six hundred to one thousand prisoners. Others were taken to the execution wall, located between block 10 and 11, and shot there. After their execution, they were burned in the crematorium at the camp.[23]

Western Europe

Meanwhile, the Nazi armies had attacked the nations of western Europe. In a series of lightning victories during 1940, the German troops took control of Denmark, Norway, Holland, Belgium, Luxembourg, and France. Suddenly the Third Reich had also acquired hundreds of thousands of additional Jews under their authority. One plan that may have been considered by some Nazis was to ship a large number of Jews out of Europe to a destination in Africa. As historian Richard Breitman pointed out, "Scholars have debated over the years whether the Nazi regime ever took seriously the idea of mass shipment of Jews to Africa."[24] Their destination was supposedly the island of Madagascar, off the coast of east Africa. According to Breitman, Himmler seemed to support a plan for the migration to Madagascar during 1940. One of his assistants, Adolf Eichmann, later said that the Jews from western Europe might have been deported to Africa, while the Jews of eastern Europe would have been killed. The reason they were to be treated differently was that the Nazis considered that the center of European Jewry was in the east. There were far more Jews there and they posed a greater threat to the Nazi regime. Thus, it was essential that the SS kill the Jews in the east.[25]

However, even those Jews going to Madagascar were not expected to survive. Hitler and Himmler both believed that fatal diseases in Africa—such as malaria—would eventually kill most of the Jews who went there. By the end of 1940, the Madagascar plan was abandoned. As Breitman explained, the process of transporting the Jews there was impossible. While the Germans had hoped to invade Great Britain and knock it out of the war, the invasion never occurred. Instead, the Germans used their air force to bomb Great Britain, hoping to convince the British to surrender. But Great Britain, led by Prime Minister Winston Churchill—who replaced Chamberlain in 1940—continued to fight. The British had a powerful navy at sea in various parts of the world. This navy would have intercepted the Nazi ships taking the Jews to Madagascar.

Therefore, Himmler and Hitler decided to turn to another solution to deal with the Jews.

6

Killing Jews in Russia

On June 22, 1941, the Nazis launched a massive invasion of the Soviet Union, called Operation Barbarossa. Although Hitler had formed an alliance with Soviet dictator Joseph Stalin in 1939, the Führer had long planned to attack the Soviet Union. He regarded the Communists as a major threat to the future of the Third Reich. Hitler also wanted the vast territory of western Russia as Lebensraum for the German people. In addition, the Nazis believed that many Soviet officials were Jews, another reason that they had to be destroyed.

Himmler and the SS were given the special assignment of killing the Communist political leaders and the Jews in the areas that were captured by the Nazis. During the summer of 1941, as 3 million German troops swept across Russian-controlled territory, vast new areas rapidly fell under Nazi control. These included eastern Poland as well as countries such as Lithuania and Latvia, which had been conquered by the Russians in 1940. No sooner had the Nazis arrived than Himmler's Einsatzgruppen appeared behind them. These Einsatzgruppen were special SS units, charged with murdering Communist officials and Jews.

At first, the Einsatzgruppen commanders acted behind the scenes. They stirred up pogroms against the Jews. In Lvov, part of Poland taken by the Russians in 1939, a pogrom was instigated by Einsatzgruppen C. This pogrom led to the murder of six thousand Jews during June and July. The Nazis herded other Jews into a ghetto created inside Lvov. Along the way, an estimated five thousand additional Jews—old people and cripples—were killed.[1] Nesse Galperin was forced to move into a ghetto in Siauliai, Lithuania. The ghetto became so overcrowded, she recalled, they were forced to live in synagogues. "With hunger, no water," she added. "They were begging for food, they were begging for them to be saved."[2] Jews were also put into prison, where they, according to one resident:

> were ordered to break concrete and dig out corpses [of people killed by the retreating Soviets]. Others were shot in the small inner courtyards of the prisons. . . . Crowds wandered along prison corridors and courtyards observing with satisfaction the suffering of the Jews. Here and there volunteers could be found to help the Germans in the beating of Jews.[3]

In Lithuania, similar pogroms began once the Nazis arrived. In the city of Kaunas (Kovno), synagogues were destroyed, Jewish homes were burned to the ground, and thousands of Jews were rounded up and held in large forts outside the city. Here they were guarded by the SS and Lithuanian partisans—soldiers allied with the Nazis. According to one observer, men, women, and children were starved to death by the Nazis and Lithuanians who worked with them. "We received strict orders to sit on the ground and not to talk. When somebody moved or was caught talking, the [Lithuanian] partisans would open automatic fire into the crowd."[4]

Himmler on the Eastern Front

Himmler had gone to the Eastern Front to direct the work of the Einsatzgruppen. He traveled in a luxurious train, called the *Heinrich*, which served as Himmler's command post. In early July, he arrived in Bialystok, a city in eastern Poland. There, seven hundred Jews had been burned alive by the Nazis in a large synagogue. Nevertheless, when Himmler arrived he criticized the work of the Einsatzgruppen for not killing more Jews, according to historian Richard Rhodes.[5]

In July, Hitler gave Himmler full control of all security measures in the east. This meant that he would direct the entire campaign to destroy the Jews. As Himmler put it:

> This is an ideological battle and a struggle of races. Here in this struggle stands National Socialism: an ideology based on the value of our Germanic, Nordic blood. Here stands a world as we have conceived it: beautiful, decent, socially equal. . . . On the other side stands a population of 180 million, a mixture of races, whose very names are unpronounceable, and whose physique is such that one can shoot them down without pity and compassion. These animals, that torture and ill-treat every prisoner from our side . . . these people have been welded by the Jews into one religion, one ideology, that is called Bolshevism [Communism] . . . [6]

According to historian Richard Breitman, Himmler planned to have his men carry out pogroms and killings of some Jews. The rest would be forced into ghettos and death camps. There they would eventually be killed to make room for more Jews being transported to the ghettos and death camps from other countries in Europe.[7]

Indeed, Jews from Holland had already been sent to the concentration camp at Mauthausen where they were killed by the SS guards. The concentration camp at Dachau was expanded. Up until 1940, prisoners died at the camp from disease or by being shot. These bodies were then put into graves. In 1940, however, the first crematorium in Nazi Germany was constructed at Dachau to burn the dead bodies. During the war on the Russian front, many prisoners were captured. These were sent to Dachau along with more Jews, who were being imprisoned there. As a result, the SS decided to expand the crematorium in 1942.

Auschwitz and the Final Solution

Meanwhile, Himmler had designated Auschwitz for a special task. Himmler met with Commandant Rudolf Höss in July 1941. According to Höss, Himmler said:

> The Führer has ordered that the Jewish question be solved once and for all and that we, the SS, are to implement that order. The existing extermination centers in the East are not in a position to carry out the large actions which are anticipated. I have therefore earmarked Auschwitz for this purpose, both because of its good position as regards communications and because the area can easily be isolated and camouflaged. . . . The Jews are the sworn enemies of the German people and must be eradicated. Every Jew that we can lay our hands on is to be destroyed now during the war without exception.[8]

According to historian Richard Breitman and other experts, this is clear proof that Hitler had already ordered the Final Solution—Endlösung—for the Jews.

Hitler did not leave any written communication about the Final Solution. However, in July 1941 Reinhard Heydrich did receive the signature of Hermann Göring, second in charge to Hitler, on an order to proceed with the Final Solution. The order stated: "I hereby charge you with making all necessary organizational, functional, and material preparations for a complete solution of the Jewish question in the German sphere of influence in Europe."[9]

Himmler's Reaction to the Final Solution

According to historian Richard Rhodes, Himmler may have experienced some misgivings about the Final Solution. During this period, his stomach problems apparently grew worse. Himmler realized that the SS had been asked by Hitler to carry out the horrible execution of millions of people across Europe. Later he compared it to the role the SS had been asked to play in the Night of the Long Knives. "It made everybody shudder," he said. Yet Himmler did not dare oppose the will of the Führer. As his physician, Dr. Felix Kersten, explained, Himmler lived to serve Hitler:

> An unfavorable comment by Hitler on one of his measures was enough to upset him thoroughly and produce violent reactions which took the form of severe stomach pains. . . . Nobody who had witnessed it would believe that a man with as much power at his disposal as Himmler would be in such a state of fear when he was summoned to Hitler. . . . This weakness of his made Himmler suffer indescribably.[10]

Although Himmler had already ordered the deaths of thousands of people, he had never actually witnessed a mass execution before August 1941. The execution was arranged at Minsk in the Ukraine, which had been overrun by the Nazis. Jews were selected by Arthur Nebe, the commander of

Himmler's Doctor

Himmler was treated for his stomach problems during the war by Dr. Felix Kersten. Born in 1898, Kersten lived in Holland. Before the war, he had become a famous physical therapist and massage expert. He treated the Dutch royal family. After Holland was conquered by the Nazis in 1940, Kersten was ordered to become Himmler's personal doctor. As the war continued, Himmler was ordering the killing of more and more Jews.

Meanwhile, the Nazi war effort was being rolled back by the Allies, and defeat became more likely. Himmler's stomach pains became much worse, and Dr. Kersten was called in more frequently to treat the Reichsführer. Kersten used his position to help save the lives of countless Jews. Kersten and his friends prepared lists of Jews to be saved. After treating Himmler, Kersten persuaded him to sign the list of Jews to be rescued from the death camps. Blank spaces were left between the names. After Himmler had put his signature on the list, Kersten added the names of more Jews. After the war ended, Kersten wrote a book about his experiences with Himmler.

Einsatzgruppe B. They were led to a ditch, ordered to get in and lie down, then they were shot by the SS. Two men, who were not killed at the first shot, especially bothered Himmler. The experience upset Himmler, who had not realized the full extent of its horror.[11] The executions were also taking a toll on the executioners. Erich von dem Bach-Zelewski, who was in charge of the guards, urged Himmler to devise a more humane way of killing the Jews—one that would spare the executioners. Indeed, some of the SS were already suffering nervous breakdowns because of their murderous work.

More Executions

The mass shootings of Jews continued. In Lithuania almost twenty-five thousand Jewish men, women, and children were massacred by the SS during August 1941. On August 31, the Nazis created an incident known as the Great Provocation. Jews were accused of firing on Nazi soldiers in the Jewish ghetto of Vilnius, Lithuania. In retaliation, thousands of Jews were rounded up and taken to Likiszki Prison. Others were forced into the ghettos at Vilnius. In early September, thousands were taken to an area outside the city, called Ponary, and shot. One woman, Sima Katz, who survived the massacre recalled that the Jews were loaded onto trucks in the middle of the night and taken to the wooded area of Ponary. At first the Jews did not know what was going to happen to them. "Suddenly the truth hit us like an electric shock," she said. "The women broke out in piteous pleas to the sentries, offering them rings and watches. Some fell to the ground and kissed the sentries' boots, others tore their hair and clothes—to no avail. The Lithuanians pushed one group after another to the site of the slaughter." Sima Katz

Considered an expert in the field of criminology, Arthur Nebe had served as head of the Prussian criminal police. He joined the SS in 1931 and was later promoted by Himmler to SS-Gruppenführer of the Criminal Police. He was also involved in the euthanasia program in Germany during the 1930s, called T–4, that was used against handicapped and mentally-ill patients. The Nazis took them to hospitals where they were killed by a lethal gas. Following the invasion of Russia, Nebe led the Einsatzgruppe B during the summer and fall of 1941. According to one estimate, this unit killed forty-five thousand Jews. As the war began to turn against the Nazis in 1943, Nebe apparently became convinced that Hitler had to be replaced. During 1944, he was involved in an attempt to assassinate the Führer. When this attempt failed, Nebe was arrested and was never seen again.

Victims of the T–4 program.

was also pushed into the ditch. Somehow she found herself underneath the bodies of other Jews, and survived.[12]

A similar event occurred southward outside of Kiev, a city in the Ukraine that had been captured by the Nazis. Jews were accused of causing explosions inside the city that killed German soldiers. As a result, on September 29–30, thousands of Jews were taken to a ravine called Babi Yar, outside of Kiev. Their clothes were removed. Then they were forced into the ravine, and thirty-three thousand of them were killed by Einsatzgruppe C. It was the worst shooting massacre of Jews during the war.

Meanwhile, the killings continued in Kaunas and other parts of Lithuania. By early December, the SS reported that over 137,000 people had been killed. One of the Einsatzgruppen leaders, Kurt Jager, confidently reported that the Jewish problem in Lithuania had been solved. He said that all of the Jews had been eliminated, except a few who had been put to work by the Nazis.[13]

In November, Himmler had ordered an end to the Jews in Riga, located in Latvia. They had to be cleared out to make room for more Jews who would be shipped there. Over ten thousand Jews were taken out to the Rumbula Forest, beyond the city. Although the weather was very cold, the Jews were forced to take off their outer clothes. They had also been ordered to put their money and jewelry in boxes that had been put on the ground to collect them. Then the Jews were herded up a hill to a pit. Six to twelve guards began to shoot them, each massacring approximately one thousand Jews. As one observer later recalled: "The victims maintained a perfect calm and composure. There were no outcries, only light sobbing and crying and soothing words to the children."[14]

In November, another massacre occurred at Slonim, located in Belorussia. The Jews there were removed to make room for others who would be shipped out from western Europe. Between nine thousand and eighteen thousand Jews were murdered by Einsatzgruppe B on November 13, 1941. One member of the Nazi unit, Alfred Metzner, later admitted: "The men, children and mothers were pushed into pits. Children were first beaten to death and then thrown feet [first] into the pits. . . . pregnant women were shot in the belly for fun and then thrown into the pits. . . . "[15]

During the invasion of the Soviet Union, the SS had already begun to implement the mass murder of Jews. According to historian Christopher Browning, there is no evidence of "a single, comprehensive killing order," coming from any top Nazi official, such as Hitler or Himmler. Nevertheless, in conversations with his commanders in the field, Himmler probably let them know what he expected. These soldiers were "expected to commence implementing the Final Solution on Soviet territory. . . ."[16]

The Concentration Camps

As the killings continued, Himmler ordered that new concentration camps be constructed. During the fall, a concentration camp at Majdanek, outside Lublin, had been started. Jews began arriving there in December. In the same area, another camp at Belzec was erected. Belzec had originally served as a labor camp in 1940. It was located near the Russian zone of Poland. Jews were ordered to build defenses to separate the Nazi zone from the Russian-controlled territory. In 1941, after the Nazis launched the invasion of Russia, the German armies took over the Russian zone in Poland. Jews were rounded up and brought to Belzec. Late in 1941, the SS began to construct gas chambers at Belzec. As one of the SS guards

recalled, the commandant of Belzec "told us that . . . 'all the Jews will be struck down.' For this purpose, barracks were built as gas chambers."[17]

The use of gas was a new form of execution for the Nazis that replaced shooting. Gas had already been used in another program that the Führer had ordered during the 1930s. This was the euthanasia—or killing—of mentally ill and handicapped people in Germany. They did not fit the Nazi description of a master race. By mid-1941, as many as seventy thousand people had already been put to death. Many of them had been killed with a lethal gas. The code name for this operation was T–4. This was the name of the street address in Berlin—Tiergartenstrasse 4—of the government office that ran the program. Early in 1941, Himmler talked to Philip Bouhler, who had been in charge of the euthanasia program. Himmler wanted to find out if the same methods could be applied to Jews in concentration camps. Bouhler sent his T–4 experts to the camps, and they began killing sick and mentally-ill Jews.

On the Eastern Front, the SS was already experimenting with gas trucks to kill Jews and other enemies of the Third Reich. The victims were forced into the back of a truck, which was then sealed. Then gas from the exhaust of the truck was piped into the sealed area, killing the victims. In December 1941, the gas trucks were used at Chelmno, a death camp in Poland. Chelmno was linked by a railroad line to Lodz, where a large Jewish ghetto had been established. After

Heinrich Himmler inspects a prisoner-of-war camp in Russia in the early 1940s.

Under Himmler's orders, concentration camps and death camps were built all over Europe.

arriving at Chelmno, Jews were usually loaded into a van. The driver of the van began pumping gas into the back. The screams of Jews filled the air, but in a short time the noise stopped because the Jews were dead. Later the van was driven to burial pits and the bodies of the Jews were dumped into a ditch that had been dug by other camp inmates. Others were burned. As one survivor recalled, "The gas vans came in here. . . . There were two huge ovens and afterward the bodies were thrown into these ovens, and the flames reached to the sky."[18]

Gas chambers were also built at Belzec. As one SS guard, Erich Fuchs, recalled: "I installed shower heads in the gas chambers. The nozzles were not connected to any water pipes; they would serve as camouflage for the gas chambers. For the Jews who were gassed it would seem as if they were being taken to baths. . . ."[19]

Another experiment with gas had begun at Auschwitz under the direction of Commandant Höss. There the prison guards had started using a pesticide—developed for killing insects and rodents—to kill prisoners. Called Zyklon B, the gas was dropped in small pellets into a sealed cell containing over eight hundred Russian prisoners and other victims. All of them were killed. Before much longer, the gas would be used to kill the Jews. Justifying the mass murders that occurred at Auschwitz and other camps, Höss later said: "It was always stressed that if Germany was to survive then World Jewry must be exterminated and we all accepted it as truth."[20]

Architect of the Holocaust

For the Jewish population of Europe, 1942 became the worst year of the Holocaust. In January, top Nazi officials met at Wannsee, a suburb of Berlin. They listened as Himmler's chief of staff, Reinhard Heydrich, instructed them to carry out the Final Solution—the murder of the Jews. Throughout much of Europe, the Final Solution had already begun. But, in 1942, the horror would grow even worse. An estimated 2.7 million Jews would be murdered—more men, women, and children losing their lives than in any other year of the Nazi terror.[1]

Many of these Jews were killed outside of Lublin. Himmler had appointed SS-Brigadeführer Odilo Globocnik and his deputy Christian Wirth to take charge of the Final Solution in that area. Wirth had been directly involved with the Nazi euthanasia program during the 1930s. He had also worked at Chelmno, setting up a gas chamber to kill the Jews who were brought to the camp. In March 1942, an estimated twenty-four thousand Jews were forcibly transported from the Lodz ghetto and killed in the gas vans at Chelmno.

Meanwhile, Himmler had directed the establishment of more death camps outside of Warsaw. He put Globocnik in charge of this task. These camps were called Sobibor and Treblinka. Jews were forced to construct their own execution facilities at Sobibor and Treblinka. These camps, in addition to Belzec, used carbon monoxide to kill their victims. Carbon monoxide worked more slowly than Zyklon B, taking about eighteen minutes to kill Jews who were exposed to it.

Transporting Jews to Their Deaths

On special trains, called Sonderzüge, Jews were carried across Europe to the death camps in the east. Driven from their homes and allowed to take only a few possessions, Jews were packed into freight cars headed for the SS camps. As one survivor recalled,

> We were packed into a closed cattle train. Inside the freight cars it was so dense that it was impossible to move. There was not enough air, many people fainted, others became hysterical. . . . In an isolated place, the train stopped. Soldiers entered the car and robbed us and even cut off fingers with rings. . . . Nobody thought about food, only about water and air. Finally we arrived at Sobibor.[2]

Other trains, with Jews packed one hundred deep in each car, traveled to Belzec and Treblinka. As the trains made their long journeys, Jews pleaded for food and water, which was not given to them by the Nazis. As a train stopped at a station along the way, some Jews tried to escape. "When a few managed to get out of the cars through the air apertures," one survivor said, "they were shot before they reached the ground. . . . By the time our train left the station, at least fifty dead women, men, and children, some of them entirely naked, were lying along the track."[3]

Eventually, the train reached Belzec. Each train included approximately forty to sixty cars. As the doors were opened, the Jews were ordered to come out of the cars by the SS guards. The SS was assisted by Jewish prisoners, called Sonderkommandos, who were forced to participate in the murder of their own people. The Sonderkommandos were led by Jews called Kapos. Some of these Jews worked on the train platforms. They brought the Jews off the trains as they arrived at the camps. They also removed the bodies of any Jews who had died during the trips. Other Sonderkommandos supervised the Jews as they undressed. A few were also in charge of collecting money or other valuables from the Jews. These valuables included watches, money, or gold. Sonderkommandos also took charge of sorting clothing that was left by the Jews after they undressed. They sorted these clothes into various piles. They also removed the bodies from the gas chambers after they were killed. Still others took the dead bodies to the burial areas.

When the new prisoners arrived at Belzec, they were herded together. Then they were addressed by Christian Wirth. He had been appointed commandant of Belzec.

Once the Jews had been assembled, they were told by Wirth that they would be taken to another location. He then explained that they must first remove their clothes to be disinfected and to take baths. Wirth and other Nazi leaders used this story so that the Jewish victims would remain quiet and subdued on their way to their murder. As one SS officer who worked at Belzec explained,

> Wirth briefed me that while I was there I should influence the Jews to behave calmly. After leaving the undressing barracks, I had to show the Jews the way

Christian Wirth

Born in 1885, Christian Wirth had served in the German army during World War I, where he fought valiantly on the Western Front. During the 1930s, he served in the police controlled by the Nazis. In 1939, Wirth went to work at a center for murdering the handicapped in Prussia. Some of the victims were mentally-ill Jews, who were gassed with carbon monoxide.

By 1940, Wirth had been promoted to inspector of many euthanasia facilities. He worked in the Lublin area with SS-Brigadeführer Odilo Globocnik and was later given the job of running Belzec. Afterward, he was put in charge of the three [death] camps—Belzec, Sobibor, and Treblinka. As one SS officer recalled: "From my activity in the [death] camps of Treblinka and Sobibor, I remember that Wirth in brutality, meanness, and ruthlessness could not be surpassed. We therefore called him 'Christian the Terrible' or 'The Wild Christian.'"[4] Later, Wirth was sent to Italy to run a concentration camp. He was killed in May 1944 in Yugoslavia.

to the gas chambers. I believe that when I showed the Jews the way they were convinced that they were really going to the baths. After the Jews entered the gas chambers, the doors were closed. . . . Then [an officer] switched on the engine which supplied the gas. After five or seven minutes—and this is only an estimate—someone looked through the small window into the gas chamber to verify whether all inside were dead. . . . The Jews inside the gas chambers were densely packed. . . . Some of them had their eyes closed, others' eyes rolled. The bodies were dragged out of the gas chambers and inspected by a dentist, who removed finger-rings and gold teeth. . . . After this procedure, the corpses were thrown into a big pit. . . .[5]

Approximately six hundred thousand Jews were killed at Belzec following the same brutal procedures. Northward at Sobibor, similar scenes were being enacted every day. Approximately two hundred fifty thousand Jews were gassed at the Sobibor death camp. As one SS guard, Kurt Bolender, later recalled,

Before the Jews undressed, Oberscharführer Michael [deputy commander] made a speech to them. On these occasions, he used to wear a white coat to give the impression [that he was] a physician. Michael announced to the Jews that they would be sent to work. But before this they would have to take baths and undergo disinfection so as to prevent the spread of diseases. . . . After undressing, the Jews . . . were led to the gas chambers. . . .[6]

Himmler and Heydrich

While the death camps outside of Warsaw were killing hundreds of thousands of Jews, the numbers of executions had also increased at Auschwitz. Commandant Höss had added additional gas chambers to handle the large numbers of Jews who were being transported to the camp. At Auschwitz,

Jews who were physically unable to work were quickly executed. Others were made to produce war matériel for the German armies, such as clothing and rubber for the tires of military vehicles.

At Auschwitz, Himmler had also given his approval to Nazi scientists to perform experiments on some of the inmates. To prevent Jewish workers from producing children in the camps, they were being sterilized. Under the direction of Professor Karl Clauberg, Jewish women were injected with a drug called formalin. These experiments occurred on Block 10 of Auschwitz, known as Clauberg's Block. Himmler was interested in knowing "how long it would take to sterilize a thousand Jewesses."[7] Other women at nearby Birkenau were sterilized using X-ray machines to destroy their ovaries. Afterward, their ovaries were removed to determine whether the X-ray treatment had worked. Many women died during these operations.

While deadly experiments were getting under way in Auschwitz, an assassination cut short the work of Himmler's chief of staff, Reinhard Heydrich. On May 27, 1942, Czech special agents ambushed Heydrich's car while he was traveling to Prague, Czechoslovakia. Heydrich was severely wounded by a bomb, and following emergency surgery, he died about a week later. Himmler rushed to his hospital bed and later delivered an oration at Heydrich's funeral. As he promised the SS leaders and other people assembled at the funeral: "The . . . Jews will be dealt with for certain in a year: then none will wander again. Because now the slate must be made quite clean."[8]

Increasing the Level of Death

In July 1942, Himmler traveled to Auschwitz to witness an execution of Jews who had been brought there from Holland.

97

Trainloads of Jews had been leaving western Europe for the death camps. They were being rounded up in Holland, Austria, and France. Then they were taken to special transit camps to await train transportation eastward. One of these camps, located at Theresienstadt, outside of Prague, had been established by Heydrich before his death. Theresienstadt was a town with a wall enclosing it. Theresienstadt became a new ghetto, where Jews were brought to await death. Approximately thirty-three thousand Jews died at Theresienstadt. About another eighty-eight thousand were shipped to the death camps.[9]

Deaths also increased at the German concentration camp at Buchenwald. Prisoners were forced to work so hard there that they died from exhaustion. As historian David Hackett later wrote,

> The stone quarry [at Buchenwald] was the truest of the "suicide" work details where several thousand comrades met their deaths through blows from stones, caning, "accidents," deliberate pushes over the precipice, shooting, and every other type of torment. A favorite practice of the sergeants was to have candidates for death, especially Jews, push an empty or even a loaded cart up a steep slope—an impossible task for one man or two prisoners together. They would be killed by the weight of the cart as it rolled back on them or by the beatings that accompanied the task.[10]

Himmler (right), Höss (third from right), and members of their inspection team arrive at the building site of the Monowitz-Buna concentration camp.

At Auschwitz, Himmler watched as the Jews were ordered out of the freight cars by SS guards and forced onto the platforms. Here some of them were selected to work at the camp, while others were taken to their deaths. These Jews were loaded onto trucks by SS guards and Jewish Sonderkommandos. Himmler went to the changing rooms, where the Jews took off their clothing and were herded into the "baths" to be washed and disinfected. Accompanied by Höss, Himmler peered through the window into the gas chamber where he could see the Jews being executed. "He viewed the extermination process in complete silence," Höss said, "saying nothing at all."[11]

From Auschwitz, Himmler journeyed eastward to Lublin. There he saw Jews being brought into the death camp at Sobibor. Himmler also ordered that all the Jews of eastern Poland should be killed by the end of 1942. This project was called Operation Reinhard, in memory of the dead Reinhard Heydrich. Indeed, Sobibor, Belzec, and Treblinka were called Operation Reinhard camps. The rate of murders was increased at these camps as well as at Majdanek, outside of Lublin. At Sachsenhausen, Dutch prisoners were executed by the SS. Hundreds of Soviet prisoners were also killed at the camp.

At Sobibor, one hundred thousand Jews were killed from early May until the close of June 1942. Once inside Sobibor, Jews were prevented from escaping by barbed-wire fences and tall watchtowers, manned by SS guards. Then the SS began to systematically murder the inmates. Some were stabbed, but many more were gassed. To increase the number of executions, the SS added more gas chambers in 1942. As prisoners arrived at the camp, they were unloaded from freight cars. Then they were taken by the SS to another camp, where the Jews were ordered to leave their belongings and undress. The guards drove them up a long enclosed passageway—called a tube—to the gas chambers. With the additional gas chambers—six in total—the Nazis could kill as many as twelve hundred Jews simultaneously.

One survivor of the camp, Kalmen Wewryk, recalled the little Jewish children who were brought there and how they were led to the gas chamber.

> There were too many Jewish children to be "processed" rapidly so they were in a long, steadily shrinking circular line from morning to night. Such beautiful children, gorgeous little blonde girls with pigtails, decently dressed. These poor unfortunates were well-fed, with pretty, round faces. . . . Many of them carried small suitcases or bags. It was pitiful, so sad! The SS men were watching over them. Some of the kids were crying. They probably understood. . . . And every minute less and less of them, less and less. The line got shorter and shorter. [They] became smoke in those accursed skies. . . ."[12]

As the Final Solution took the lives of more and more Jews, Himmler worked harder and harder to supervise the entire program. His day began early in the morning and continued until two or three the following morning. This left him little time for sleep. He traveled continually from one death camp to another. At these camps he witnessed the death of Jews, met with the SS soldiers in charge of the camps, and read hundreds of reports.[13]

Among the camps that Himmler supervised was Treblinka. Treblinka had begun its executions in July 1942, with approximately two hundred thousand Jews killed there by the beginning of September. Abraham Bomba, a survivor of the camp, worked at Treblinka. He had no idea what was happening at the camp when he first arrived:

> I couldn't believe what had happened over there on the other side of the gate, where the people went in,

> everything disappeared, and everything got quiet. . . .
> when we start to ask the people who worked here before
> us what had happened to the others, they said: 'What do
> you mean, what happened? Don't you know that?
> They're all gassed, all killed.[14]

By the fall of 1943, when Treblinka closed, as many as nine hundred thousand Jews would be killed there.

Jews were shipped to Treblinka along a railroad line that ran from the Warsaw ghetto. As a member of the SS, Franz Suchomel, recalled, "while five thousand Jews arrived in Treblinka, three thousand were dead in the cars. They had slashed their wrists, or just died. We stacked them. . . . Thousands of people piled one on top of another on the ramp." Others were taken to the gas chambers.

> The smell was infernal because gas was constantly
> escaping. . . . More people kept coming, always more,
> whom we hadn't the facilities to kill. The brass was in a
> rush to clean out the Warsaw ghetto. The gas chambers
> couldn't handle the load. The small gas chambers. The
> Jews had to wait their turn for a day, two days, three
> days. They foresaw what was coming. They foresaw it.[15]

By this time, conditions inside the Warsaw ghetto had become even more desperate. Many Jews were suffering from starvation. The Nazis provided them with only about 180 calories of food per day.[16] Others were dying from tuberculosis—a fatal disease that infects the human lungs.

On the night of April 18, 1942, fifty Jews had been murdered by the Nazis—an event that was called "The Night of Blood." Adam Czerniakow, a Jewish leader of the Warsaw ghetto, was ordered by the Nazis to select Jews to be "resettled." By this time the Jews living in Warsaw knew that "resettled" simply meant that they were to be executed at one of the death camps. Czerniakow refused to assist the

Franz Stangl

Franz Stangl was born in 1908 in Austria. He became a policeman in 1931, and a short time later joined the Nazi party. Stangl had been the first Commandant at Sobibor. Later he was transferred to Treblinka, overseeing the execution of the Jews. Prisoners saw him regularly, in his unusual uniform of white horseback-riding clothes. Stangl believed that he was simply carrying out the orders of Reichsführer-SS Himmler. Nevertheless, he intended to do his job effectively. He later estimated that as many as twelve thousand to fifteen thousand Jews were routinely murdered in a single fourteen-hour day. "That was my profession," he admitted. "I enjoyed it. It fulfilled me. And yes, I was ambitious about that, I won't deny it." Asked about his responsibility for the deaths of so many people, Stangl later said:

> To tell the truth, one did become used to it . . . they were cargo. I think it started the day I first saw the . . . [killing area] in Treblinka. I remember [Christian] Wirth standing there, next to the pits full of blue-black corpses. It had nothing to do with humanity—it could not have. It was a mass—a mass of rotting flesh.[17]

At the end of the war, Stangl escaped from Germany. However, he was captured in Brazil in 1967. In Germany, he was tried and sent to prison for life. He died shortly afterward.

Germans and instead committed suicide. In his suicide note, he said, "I am powerless . . . I can no longer bear this."[18] Thousands of Jews were taken from their homes by the Nazis, and a majority sent to Treblinka.

Throughout the remainder of 1942, the execution of Jews continued. By the end of July, reports from General-kommisar Wilhelm Kube in Belorussia told a horrifying story. Gas trucks had been used to kill fifty-five thousand Jews. Approximately ten thousand had been killed in Minsk at the end of July. Approximately twenty-four thousand had been murdered in Lida and Slonim in Poland.[19] In August, hundreds of Jews were shot in Radom, Poland, while many more were shipped to Treblinka.

During early September, the SS gathered up the Jews of Dzialoszyce, Poland, killing some of them in a cemetery and taking the rest to Belzec for execution. Similar executions were repeated in the Ukraine, Lublin, and Warsaw. Late in October, sixteen thousand Jews were shot to death in Pinsk, Poland. During the first week of November, the combined death toll at Belzec, Auschwitz, and Treblinka reached one hundred seventy thousand in a single seven-day period. Meanwhile, Jews were being transported in increasing numbers to the death camps from western Europe.

The world had never experienced such wholesale mass murder. Yet, as Himmler told his officers in 1943,

> Most of you must know what it means to see a hundred corpses lie side by side, or five hundred, or a thousand. To have stuck this out and . . . to have kept our integrity, that is what has made us hard. In our history, this is an unwritten and never-to-be-written page of glory. We have carried out this heaviest of our tasks in a spirit of love for our people. And our inward being, our soul, our character has not suffered injury from it.[20]

8

Himmler Increases the Jewish Terror

In January 1943, Field Marshal Friedrich von Paulus, commanding the German Sixth Army, prepared to surrender at Stalingrad—a major city in Russia. His soldiers had been surrounded by Soviet armies. As Paulus put it: "As commander of an army what should I say when a man comes to me and begs: Herr Colonel-General, a piece of bread? It's already the fourth day on which the men have had nothing to eat. . . . We can't retake a position any more, because the men are collapsing with exhaustion."[1] The Nazi defeat at Stalingrad marked a turning point of World War II. Hitler's dream of conquering Russia was over, and the German armies would continue to retreat all the way to Berlin.

The Nazi defeat, however, did not stop Himmler's efforts to round up Jews and send them off to death camps. Indeed, as historian Donald McKale wrote: "Instead, as far as the

Nazi leadership was concerned, the problems in the war seemed only to make Germany's most critical wartime task, the extermination of the Jews, more urgent."[2] Although Himmler recognized that trains were necessary to bring more troops to the Eastern Front, he did not hesitate to telegraph the transportation department, demanding more help in transporting Jews to the concentration camps. "I need your help and support," he wrote. "If I am to wind things up quickly, I must have more trains for transports. I know very well how taxing the situation is for the railways and what demands are constantly made of you. Just the same, I must make this request: help me get more trains."[3] Himmler received them.

A survey, ordered by Himmler in 1943, revealed that 3.1 million Jews had already been killed. But there were still millions of other Jews to be removed. Some of them, however, Himmler planned to keep alive. He had received Hitler's approval to save wealthy, powerful Jews. Since they had friends in the United States, these Jews might be used as "bargaining chips" to persuade the Allies to make peace. In April 1943, Himmler ordered the construction of a special concentration camp for them at Bergen-Belsen in Germany. The first commandant of the camp was Adolf Haas. Later he was replaced by SS-Hauptsturmführer Josef Kramer. He was a veteran of the concentration camps. Kramer was later called the "Beast of Belsen" because of his especially inhuman treatment of prisoners there. As one Jewish prisoner recalled, "A strange gleam lurked in his small eyes, and he worked like a madman. I saw him throw himself at one unfortunate woman and with a single stroke of his truncheon [heavy stick] shatter her skull. . . ."[4] Prisoners were never gassed at Bergen-Belsen. They were taken to other death camps to be gassed.

The Death Camps

Other Jews were taken to death camps in the west. These included Sachsenhausen, a camp located near Berlin. As Anton Kaindl, the commandant at the camp, later revealed,

> . . . prisoners were killed by shooting or hanging. For the mass exterminations, we used a special room in the infirmary. There was a height gauge and a table with an eye scope. There were also some SS wearing doctor uniforms. There was a hole at the back of the height gauge. While a SS was measuring the height of a prisoner, another one placed his gun in the hole and killed him by shooting in his neck. Behind the height gauge there was another room where we played music in order to cover the noise of the shooting.[5]

According to Kaindl, forty-two thousand prisoners were killed while he was in command at Sachsenhausen.

Similar scenes were occurring at Mauthausen, inside Austria. At Mauthausen, the SS regularly doused inmates with water and let them stand outside in the cold winter weather until they froze to death. Eventually, a gas chamber that looked like a bathroom was added. According to Franz Ziereis, the commander of the camp, Himmler once appeared at Mauthausen to participate in the killing of an inmate. He told the SS guards to put a heavy stone on a Jew's back and force him to run with it, until he collapsed and died. Other inmates were shot by the SS, while still others were destroyed by a large German dog that chewed them apart. In 1943, Himmler witnessed the shooting of fifty Russian prisoners of war at Mauthausen.

Meanwhile, Himmler was trying to persuade his camp commandants to drive prisoners harder to produce more war matériel. As German armies were pressed harder by the Russian troops in the Soviet Union, the need for more war

supplies grew. Himmler wanted the prisoners in his camps to manufacture more airplane parts, hand grenades, rifles, and shells.

At Ravensbrück, the camp built for women prisoners in Germany, the number of inmates rose to forty-two thousand during 1943. Some of the women were strong enough to work. Those who were unable to work were shot or hanged by the SS guards. Others were transferred to a nearby camp called Uckermark. Here they were put into the vans of trucks, sealed inside, and gassed with exhaust fumes. They were dead in fifteen to twenty minutes. Women who gave birth to children at Ravensbrück were immediately stripped of their babies. The SS guards then drowned the newborns, while the mothers were forced to witness the deaths of their children. Approximately ninety-two thousand inmates were eventually killed at Ravensbrück.

The executions also continued at Chelmno. Jews arrived from Lodz. They had been misled by the SS into thinking that they would be working for the Nazis in the war effort. Trains from Lodz regularly carried twenty to twenty-two cars. The Jews were then transported to the village of Zawadki, not far from Chelmno. Here they were put up for the night inside a large mill. The next day, three trucks would take one hundred or more Jews to Chelmno. Here they were gassed. Then the trucks would come back for another load. In this

Heinrich Himmler (with back to car door) arrives at the concentration camp near Stutthof, Poland. By the end of the war, 65,000 prisoners had died at the camp. One Nazi scientist had inmates killed so he could make soap from their body fat.

way, the new load of Jews did not know what was going to happen to them. Jews at Chelmno were killed by being locked into vehicles and gassed with carbon monoxide. Then their bodies were burned.[6]

Revolts by the Jews

The task of transporting Jews to the death camps was becoming more and more difficult for the SS. By 1943, many Jews realized that transportation from the ghettos meant that they were being taken to their deaths. During the previous year, many Jews had been taken from the ghetto at Czestochowa, Poland, to the death camp at Treblinka. In January 1943, a revolt broke out in the ghetto when the SS tried to take more Jews. Although the Jewish Fighting Organization tried to stop the Nazis, the Jews were overpowered by German firepower. After the revolt was put down, over 375 Jews—including children and old people—were executed by the Nazis.

Nevertheless, a similar revolt occurred at Minsk Mazowiecki, near Warsaw. The Nazis intended to destroy the entire Jewish ghetto and take all the Jews to a death camp. This revolt was also put down, and the Jewish leaders burned to death after they had taken refuge inside a school. In February, another revolt broke out in the Bialystok ghetto. After the revolt ended, the SS executed two thousand and sent almost ten thousand others to Treblinka.[7]

Some Jewish prisoners tried to escape on the train rides from the ghettos to the death camps. A few cut their way through the barbed wire that had been placed over the small windows in the freight cars. Then they jumped out as the trains were moving. Others broke through the wooden sides of the freight cars and made their escapes. Few of these escapes, however, were successful. Jews who left the trains were hunted down and shot by the SS. Those who eluded the guards and asked for help from local farmers were generally turned away. Some found their way back to the ghettos where they continued to hide from the SS.

In August 1943, a second revolt broke out in Bialystock, Poland. Jay M., a resident of the ghetto, recalled how the uprising there began.

> . . . it was announced that the whole population of the ghetto is going to be moved. Of course, everybody knew what it meant: it's going to be the end [at the death camps]. Shooting started, and all the Germans that were then in the ghetto opened fire on everybody. The house [where he was living] was littered with bullets. . . . Briefly looking out through one of the windows, in the backyard I saw a great number of people there . . . hiding in the bushes and trees. One German walked in with a submachine gun and just sprayed bullets, and everybody was falling like little wooden soldiers.[8]

Another soldier came into the house where Jay was hiding. But he hid under the bed and was not discovered.

Many Jews who were not killed were transported to the death camps. There were attempted escapes from the camps. Individual inmates from camps such as Treblinka, Chelmno, and Sobibor tried to slip past the guards at night. But the SS strengthened the camp defenses against escapes. Mines were laid outside the camp at Chelmno. Additional barbed-wire fences were placed around the camps, and more towers were built and manned with guards. Most of the escapees were caught and executed.

The Warsaw Ghetto

By the middle of 1943, Himmler was putting in long hours trying to round up as many Jews as possible for the death camps. His doctor, Felix Kersten, tried to persuade Himmler to cut down his hours of work because it seemed to be jeopardizing his health. However, Himmler would not listen. "History will not enquire how well Heinrich Himmler slept," he said, "but how much he achieved."[9] In February 1943, Himmler ordered that the sixty thousand Jews who still lived in the Warsaw ghetto should be sent to the death camps and the ghetto destroyed. During the previous year, the Nazis had already taken hundreds of thousands of Jews to Treblinka. The remaining Jews in Warsaw knew what was happening at Treblinka. As a result, the Jewish Fighting Organization, led by Mordecai Anielewicz, recruited more Jews who were willing to stand up to the Nazis. They felt that they "had nothing to lose," according to historian Donald McKale.[10]

Under the command of SS-Brigadeführer Jürgen Stroop, ordered to Warsaw by Himmler, the SS struck the ghetto early in the morning of April 19. This was the day before Passover, a Jewish religious holiday. As the SS troops entered the ghetto, they were ambushed by the Jewish resistance fighters, who used homemade bombs, called Molotov cocktails. The SS was forced to retreat. Himmler was furious when he heard that the mission had not been successful.[11] He ordered Stroop to continue the battle.

Day after day, the SS continued to assault the ghetto, where they were met by the Jewish resistance using a few pistols and rifles. The Jews hid in the Warsaw sewer system, making it difficult for the SS to find them. Stroop then set fire to the buildings, where some of the resistance had holed up for protection. As Jews escaped from the buildings, some were shot while others were captured and taken to Treblinka. The battle raged throughout the rest of April and throughout much of May. Anielewicz and some of his men were killed on

May 8, when the Nazis attacked their position in the Warsaw ghetto. Before he died, Anielewicz had written: "My life's dream has come true; I have lived to see Jewish resistance in the ghetto in all its greatness and glory."[12] Many of the Jews were killed, while approximately fifty-six thousand were captured. Some were shot, while the rest were shipped to Treblinka. Finally, Stroop announced, "The Jewish Quarter of Warsaw is no more."[13]

Revolts at the Death Camps

When the Jews deported from Warsaw arrived at Treblinka, they found that a group of prisoners there were planning a mass escape from the death camp. One member of the group planning the escape had obtained a key to a storeroom where the SS kept a supply of rifles. The prisoners also intended to use axes and shovels that they had been given by the guards to work around the camp. With these tools, they hoped to surprise the guards, kill them, then steal any weapons that they were holding. When the prisoners at Treblinka heard about the Warsaw uprising, they had a mixed reaction. Some felt that if they revolted, the same fate would await them—death by the SS. Others believed that since the Jews were courageous enough to stand up to the Nazis at Warsaw, those at Treblinka should do the same thing.

By July, the prisoners realized that the need for Treblinka was growing less important. So many Jews had already been gassed, that fewer and fewer prisoners were arriving at Treblinka. In addition, the prisoners had almost finished their work cremating the bodies of the Jews who had been killed there. Himmler had ordered the cremation to cover up any evidence of the executions. As a result, those who were left there feared that the camp would be torn down and they would be executed.[14]

113

The revolt was launched on August 2, 1943. The SS weapons were secretly taken from the storeroom. The Jews took over the killing area of the camp and began burning the wooden buildings there. Then they began to head for the fences around the camp. They cut the fences with axes, put blankets over the barbed wire outside, and began to climb over it. By this time, however, the guards in the towers around the camp began shooting at the escaping prisoners. Nevertheless, some of them made good in their escape. About one hundred prisoners entered the nearby woods where they eluded the Nazis and fled to Warsaw. A much larger number, about four hundred, were killed at the camp. About one hundred others were rounded up by the SS, after they had called in reinforcements. As one fugitive, Yechiel Reichman, recalled, "the murderers were chasing us with their machine-gun fire. Simultaneously a car was pursuing us, a machine-gun firing from its roof. Many of us fell. The dead were scattered everywhere. I ran to the left, while the car stayed on the road, firing." Eventually, Reichman escaped into the woods.[15]

A similar revolt occurred at Sobibor. The prisoners there also believed that their work was almost done and the remaining inmates would soon be liquidated by the SS. Belzec had already been destroyed. The remaining Jews, about six hundred of them, were brought to Sobibor and killed by the Nazis in June. The Jews at Sobibor did not want to suffer the same fate.

Planning for the revolt at Sobibor took place over the next few months. The revolt was led by Lieutenant Alexander Pechersky, a Russian soldier. Finally, on October 14, the uprising began. SS men were lured by the prisoners into warehouses, where clothes were kept from Jews who had been gassed at the camp. One guard was told by Jewish workers that they had discovered a special coat for him. After he came in, he was attacked and killed. The deputy commander of the camp was killed in the tailor shop, when he was trying on a new uniform made for him by an inmate. Another officer, in charge of the camp guards, was killed in a similar way. As Yehuda Lerner, a prisoner, later explained:

> . . . the German entered that I and my friend awaited. He said that he hoped his winter overcoat was ready. The tailor brought the coat and started to fit it on him. It turned out that the German was closer to me than to my friend. I was sitting and sewing a button on a coat . . . and the axe was between my legs. I got up, keeping the coat over the axe, approached the SS man from behind and split his head. . . .[16]

Other SS guards were also overpowered and killed.

Prisoners made for the barbed-wire fences and the minefields that surrounded the camp. Many were killed, but others were able to cross over the bodies of their fallen comrades. About three hundred Jews escaped from Sobibor. Only one hundred were ever captured.

Himmler's Response

In 1943, Himmler had been promoted by Hitler to the position of Interior Minister, in recognition of his efforts to implement the Final Solution. He had not expected that the Jews would strike back as they had at Sobibor and Treblinka. He feared that the same thing might happen at other camps in the area where Jews worked as slaves in Nazi war industries. In an operation called Erntefest—Harvest Festival—he ordered that all of these Jews should be killed. On November 3, at Poniatowa labor camp in Poland, fifteen thousand Jews were taken out to dig trenches. Then they were shot and their bodies fell into the trenches. At Trawniki, another Polish labor camp, the same thing was repeated. Eight thousand to ten thousand Jews were massacred. Finally, at Majdanek on November 3, eighteen thousand Jews were killed, while loud music played to cover up their screaming.

Meanwhile, Himmler ordered the destruction of the Jewish ghetto at Bialystok. These Jews were transported to Treblinka and killed. Treblinka was then shut down in November, followed by Sobibor.

The Death Camp at Auschwitz

While Himmler ordered the destruction of some of the concentration camps, the operations at Auschwitz were expanded. In 1942, Auschwitz II—called Birkenau—had already begun operations, killing a large number of Jews. During 1943, four new gas chambers were delivered to Auschwitz-Birkenau. Each new gas chamber could kill an estimated two thousand Jews in twenty minutes. After the Jews were gassed, their bodies were sent to crematoriums, each of which could burn twenty-five hundred corpses per day.[17] By the end of 1943, there were over eighty-seven thousand prisoners at Auschwitz, double the number who had been there earlier in the year. Jews were rounded up in France and shipped by train to the Auschwitz death camp. Jews also came from Holland, Italy, and Czechoslovakia.

As a child, Judith Jaegermann was taken to the camp at Theresienstadt in Czechoslovakia and then to Auschwitz. She remembers being forced into a cattle car while being watched by Adolf Eichmann. On the way to the death camp, her father asked one of the guards where they would be transported afterward. He replied by putting a thumb up in the air. "Sure, to up there, through the chimney, which is burning 24 hours a day. . . ." After arriving at Auschwitz at night, Judith and her family were forced out of the railroad

Rudolf Höss

As commandant of Auschwitz, Himmler appointed Rudolf Höss. Born in Baden-Baden, Germany, in 1900, Höss grew up under the watchful eye of an authoritative father. As Höss later put it, "It was constantly impressed upon me in forceful terms that I must obey promptly the wishes and commands of my parents." According to historian Joachim Fest, obedience to authority was the ruling principle of Höss' life.

He served in the German army during World War I, where he was awarded medals for bravery. After the war he joined the Freikorps, just like Heinrich Himmler. In 1934, Höss became a member of the SS. He first served at Dachau, where he witnessed the brutal treatment of the prisoners there. In 1940, he became commandant of Auschwitz.

Höss apparently did not feel badly about killing so many Jews, saying he "had really never wasted much thought on it." However, he added, "I always shuddered at the prospect of carrying out extermination by shooting, when I thought of the vast numbers concerned, and of the women and children." It was easier for him to use the gas chambers. However, he pointed out: "Believe me it wasn't always a pleasure to see the mountains of corpses and smell the perpetual burning." As Fest emphasizes, Höss was proud of his work at Auschwitz, saying it could kill far more people than Treblinka.[18] After the war, Höss was tried and executed in 1947.

car, under the glare of harsh lights. They were tattooed with numbers, like many other prisoners in the death camp. Her number was 71502. "It was very painful and when I wanted to take my hand away because it hurt, I was given a slap in the face. It was a big, ugly Polish woman who did the tattooing." She was taken to Birkenau, along with other prisoners. They received very little food and soon became extremely thin. During the cold weather there, Judith developed frostbite on her feet, which were infected. Those people who could not withstand the harsh conditions were shot by the SS guards. Or they were taken to the gas chambers.[19] In charge of deciding who should live and who should die was one of the Nazi doctors. His name was Josef Mengele.

At Auschwitz, Sonderkommandos were forced to take the dead bodies out of the gas chambers after they died. A Czech Jew, Filip Muller, had heard the Jews dying inside the gas chambers. "After a while I heard the sound of piercing screams, banging against the door and also moaning and wailing. People began to cough. Their coughing grew worse from minute to minute, a sign that the gas had started to act."[20] After the Jews had been killed, Muller and other members of the Sonderkommandos opened their mouths to look for gold fillings. These were extracted and collected. Then the bodies were taken to the ovens to be burned. As Muller recalled: "I entered the cremation chamber. There was a Jewish prisoner, Fischel. . . . He looked at me, and I watched him poke the fire with a long rod. He told me: 'Do as I'm doing, or the SS will kill you.' I picked up a steel poker and did as he was doing." Later that day, there was a malfunction in the ovens and the Sonderkommandos stopped working. "That evening some trucks came," Muller continued, "and we had to load the rest, some three hundred bodies, into the trucks. . . . We were ordered to unload the bodies and put them in a pit."[21]

From January 1943 until the end of 1944, an estimated eight hundred fifty thousand Jews were killed at Auschwitz. Himmler recognized that his SS men had been called upon to do a harsh job. But, as he told them, "To be harsh towards ourselves and others, to give death and to take it" was their motto. He added: "We must forswear and renounce false comradeship, falsely conceived compassion, false softness, and a false excuse to ourselves." Himmler convinced himself that he was doing this work for the Führer, and his role was to be, according to historian Joachim Fest, "that he was the most extreme SS man among the Führer's followers."[22]

9

Last Year in Power

Throughout 1944, Heinrich Himmler's trains kept carrying Jewish prisoners to the concentration camps inside the Third Reich. In early February, more than twelve hundred Jews from France were taken to Auschwitz. Almost one thousand of them were executed in the gas chambers, including almost two hundred children.[1]

However, time was rapidly running out for the Nazis. Soviet armies were pushing farther and farther westward, bringing them ever closer to the borders of the Third Reich. The Nazi high command feared that with their defeats on the battlefield, the Hungarian government—a longtime ally— might decide to drop out of the war. In March, the Nazis took control of Hungary. Under the direction of Himmler and Adolf Eichmann, the SS began to round up the Hungarian Jews. In the past, the government of Hungary had refused to turn them over to the Nazis.

Adolf Eichmann

Born in Germany in 1906, Adolf Eichmann was taken by his family to Austria as a child. Later, he joined the Nazi party and took charge of the Austrian office of Jewish emigration in 1938. In 1941, Eichmann attended the Wannsee Conference where the SS discussed the general orders to implement the Final Solution. There, he was told by Heydrich that Himmler had called for an end to all emigration by Jews.

In 1941, Eichmann brought a message from Reinhard Heydrich to liquidate the Jewish ghetto at Lublin. That same year, he witnessed the execution of five thousand Jews at Minsk. Later he said, "It was impressive to see them all jumping into the pit without offering any resistance whatsoever. Then the men of the [SS] squad banged away into the pit with their rifles and machine pistols."[2] Eichmann ordered millions of Jews transported to the death camps.

Eichmann visited Auschwitz where he said Commandant Höss told him that Himmler, touring the camp, had declared that this was a "bloody fight which our coming generations would need to fight no more."[3] In 1944, Eichmann took charge of moving several hundred thousand Hungarian Jews to Auschwitz. Eichmann escaped from Germany at the end of the war, but he was later captured in Argentina. In 1960, he stood trial in Israel for crimes against humanity. Eichmann was found guilty and executed in 1962.

In Hungary, there were approximately seven hundred fifty thousand Jews, the largest Jewish community that had escaped the Holocaust. In April, eighteen hundred Hungarian Jews arrived in Auschwitz. By the end of June, almost four hundred thousand Hungarian Jews had been transported to the death camp. Alexander Ehrmann and his family were in this group. Arriving in Auschwitz, the family was separated at the whim of Dr. Mengele. Alexander, his father, and two sisters were spared. His mother and older sister along with her child were ordered to the gas chambers. Later, Alexander Ehrmann recalled:

> We were walking, and beyond the barbed wire fences there were piles of rubble and branches, pine tree branches and rubble burning, slowly burning. . . . I heard a baby crying. The baby was crying somewhere in the distance and I couldn't stop and look. We moved, and it smelled, a horrible stench. I knew that things in the fire were moving, there were babies in the fire.[4]

Jews who were not executed were put to work in the factories at Auschwitz turning out war matériel for the Nazis. The need was becoming more desperate for the German armies who were running short of supplies. Jews were driven like slaves, working longer and longer hours. They turned out electrical gear for planes and ships and clothing for German soldiers.

At the same time, other Jews became the special project of Dr. Mengele. He was performing experiments on twins. Among them were Vera Kriegel and her sister Olga—five-year-old children. "They injected our eyes with liquid that burnt," she said. "But we tried to remain strong, because we knew that in Auschwitz the weak went 'up the chimney.'" Others did not survive the experiments.[5]

As Russian armies swept toward the Baltic, Himmler stepped up his efforts to eliminate the remaining Jews. During March 1944, Jewish children from Kaunas were dragged from their homes by the SS and shot. As one observer later recalled,

> I saw mothers screaming. A mother whose three children had been taken away—she went up to this automobile and shouted at the German, "Give me the children," and he said, "How many?" and the German said, "You may have one." . . . and all three children looked at her and stretched out their hands. Of course, all of them wanted to go with the mother, and the mother didn't know which child to select, and she went down alone, and she left the car.[6]

In June 1944, the Russian armies drew close to the work camp at Maly Trostinets outside Minsk. Before leaving the camp, the SS rounded up the Jews and other prisoners, forced them into a building, and burned it to the ground. A similar event occurred at Vilna in July. Most of the Jews working at a Nazi factory were taken out and shot before the Russians could arrive.

Although Himmler knew the war was lost, he intended to finish the job he had started—the Final Solution. As historians Deborah Dwork and Robert Jan van Pelt have written, "Previously the 'solution' had been a means to an end." Himmler had intended to move Germans to the areas where Jews had lived in Poland and Russia. German farmers would settle there and "create a racially pure, unified German nation, [Himmler's] utopia of German blood working German soil." But as the Nazis retreated, this "dream" had become impossible. "But now, getting rid of the Jews, cleansing Europe of them, was an end in itself. No longer part of a larger program, it was a project on its own."[7]

At Chelmno, for example, the pace of the killing intensified. An estimated ten thousand prisoners were killed in 1944. Across Europe, the Nazis killed a total of over six hundred thousand Jews.[8]

Himmler and Hitler

Himmler and Hitler were united in their effort to rid Europe of Jews. But the war had taken a terrible toll on Hitler. In 1939, he had been a vigorous leader, directing his troops into Poland and the following year into western Europe. By 1944, however, many people who saw Hitler described him as looking like an old man. He did not walk upright but stooped over. One of his hands and arms shook. The dynamic leader of the past had gone.

Some of Hitler's supporters, including prominent generals in the armed forces, now believed that the Nazi Führer was leading Germany to its ruin. These men mounted a plot to assassinate Hitler and bring an immediate end to the war. On July 20, 1944, one of the conspirators, Klaus von Stauffenberg, attended a high-level meeting at Hitler's headquarters. It was called the Wolf's Lair, in East Prussia. Stauffenberg placed a bomb, hidden in his briefcase, under the table where Hitler was looking at his maps of the war. Shortly afterward, Stauffenberg left the room and the bomb exploded. While Hitler was injured, he was not killed.

According to Himmler's biographer Peter Padfield, the Reichsführer-SS probably knew about the plot. His SS operatives roamed at will throughout the Third Reich. They listened in on conversations and opened mail. They arrested suspected enemies of the Third Reich and tortured them. Then they brought their information to Himmler. He had also developed doubts about Hitler's leadership. However, Himmler planned to take no steps against the Führer.

Hedwig Potthast

During World War II, Himmler and his wife, Marga, grew apart from each other and spent little time together. Meanwhile, Himmler had developed a relationship with his secretary, Hedwig Potthast. Born in 1912, Hedwig was twelve years younger than Himmler. Her father had been a sergeant in the German army. She went to work for Himmler before the beginning of World War II. Himmler built a house for Hedwig and spent much of his time with her. On February 15, 1942, the couple had a son, named Helge. Two years later, Hedwig gave birth to a daughter, Nanette. The birth occurred on July 20, 1944, the same day of the attempted assassination of Adolf Hitler.

As the war grew worse for the Nazis, Himmler found a comfortable retreat at Hedwig's house. In the fall, he spent time playing with his children and putting up pictures on the walls. In early 1945, as the Soviet armies moved closer to Berlin, Hedwig and the two children were taken out of the city. Himmler hid out with them after Berlin fell to the Soviet armies in May 1945.

Instead, he had decided to wait and see what happened.[9] When Himmler realized that the Führer had survived the assassination attempt, he rushed to the Wolf's Lair. He also ordered the arrest of von Stauffenberg.

Hitler never seems to have doubted Himmler's loyalty. Perhaps he should have been more suspicious. According to historian Hugh Thomas, as early as 1943, Himmler's agents were in contact with American agents. Proposals were discussed that called for Himmler to take over as leader of Germany. Peace would then be made with the western Allies, while the Nazis continued to wage war against the Communist government in the Soviet Union. But the Führer seemed unaware of these conversations.[10] Indeed, Hitler appointed Himmler to a new position in 1944—Chief of German Armaments and Commander of the Home Army, defending the German borders. Himmler replaced one of the generals who had been involved in the plot against Hitler. In his new position, Himmler continued to work side by side with Hitler, even as the fortunes of the Third Reich continued to fall.

Revolt in Warsaw and Auschwitz

In the west, Allied troops had landed in France a month before the assassination attempt on Hitler. After the landings on June 6, 1944, called D-Day, the Allies began to advance across western Europe. In the east, Russian troops were nearing Warsaw. Late in July, they forced the Nazis to abandon the death camp at Majdanek. As the Soviet armies approached Warsaw, Polish freedom fighters decided to stage a revolt against the Nazis occupying the city. The Poles hoped that they would receive help from the Soviet armies. As the revolt broke out, Himmler ordered that the Poles should be crushed and the city of Warsaw destroyed. Nazi tanks and heavy artillery leveled the city, while German soldiers burned out the Polish residents. As Himmler told members of the German army, "You may think I am a frightful barbarian. I am, I may say, if I have no other choice."[11] As Himmler brutally stamped out the Warsaw revolt, Soviet troops made no effort to help the Poles. Stalin had decided to let Warsaw be destroyed by the Nazis. This made it easier for the Soviet armies to take control of the city after the Germans retreated.

Meanwhile, Himmler also continued to worry about the future of the Third Reich. To protect himself, he issued an order in September 1944, saying, "I forbid any liquidation of Jews, and order that on the contrary, care should be given to weak and sick persons." According to historian Hugh Thomas, this order was given to put Himmler in the best light with the western Allies.[12]

North of Warsaw, the Russian armies drew near Lodz. Before evacuating the city, the Nazis decided to destroy the Jewish ghetto. The more than sixty thousand Jews still remaining in Lodz were loaded onto trains and shipped to the death camp at Auschwitz. Jews were also being sent to Auschwitz from the ghetto at Theresienstadt in Czechoslovakia. Approximately sixty-five hundred were sent to the camp in late September and early October. Many were killed in the gas chambers. As the war drew to a close, the SS began to destroy the records of the deaths at Auschwitz to conceal what had happened there.

At Auschwitz, the Jewish Sonderkommandos had decided to stage a revolt against the SS. They had smuggled in a few explosives but had very few arms to use against the SS guards. However, the Jews feared that plans were already under way to destroy Auschwitz as the Soviets drew closer to the camp. This would mean that the Jews would be killed. Indeed, some of them had already been gassed in September.

On October 7, a revolt broke out at one of the crematoriums. Using axes and crowbars, the Jewish workers wounded some of the SS guards. Others began firing at the Jews. While some of the Jews were killed, others escaped. SS guards, strengthened with reinforcements, pursued the escaped prisoners. All of them were eventually killed.

Last Days of the Third Reich

By the end of 1944, Heinrich Himmler was considered the most powerful man in the Third Reich, after Hitler.[13] Himmler had control of the SS and directed the home army and military armaments used to defend Germany. He had created a powerful empire. It included the Gestapo, who could arrest anyone at will throughout the Third Reich. Himmler's empire was defended by the Waffen-SS soldiers. These troops had also distinguished themselves in the fighting on the Eastern Front and during the retreat across western Europe. Indeed, Hitler regarded them as among his most reliable soldiers.

Himmler also directed the SS guards who ran the concentration camps—men who led prisoners to the gas chambers. From his office in Berlin, the Reichsführer-SS guided the day-to-day decisions that led to the murder of millions of Jews and other prisoners. And, with a single order, Himmler could bring about the destruction of a city.

However, Himmler's loyalty to the Führer had continued to waver. During the fall, Himmler had contacted the British, hoping to negotiate a peace with them on the Western Front. Himmler believed that the British and Americans would welcome the support of the Nazis to hold back the Communists in the Soviet Union. He saw the Nazis as the most powerful bulwark against Bolshevism. Himmler did not understand that the Allies wanted nothing to do with him. His role in the murder of Jews and other prisoners was already widely known.[14] Nevertheless, Himmler continued his efforts to interest the western Allies in dealing with him.

Himmler offered to release some prominent Jews in return for substantial payoffs. In the fall, he also ordered an end to the murders at Auschwitz. Nevertheless, the murders there continued. By this time, the SS guards feared for their own futures at the hands of prisoners who might revolt at the camps. They felt that the only way to avoid this problem was to kill all of them.

In January 1945, as Soviet forces approached Auschwitz, many of the remaining Jews were forced to leave the camp on foot. The Jews on these death marches numbered about sixty thousand.[15] The SS intended to bring them to other camps inside Germany. Some Jews were shot along the way because they were too weak to travel. "We heard shooting all the time," one prisoner recalled. "We were not allowed to turn our heads, but we knew what the shooting meant. All those lagging behind were shot dead."[16]

Many sick Jewish prisoners, however, were left at Auschwitz. Among the prisoners remaining at Auschwitz was an Italian chemist named Primo Levi. As Levi came out from the cold barracks, he was surprised to find that the "Germans were no longer there. The towers were empty." Levi went out to look around the camp. "The camp guards must have left in a great hurry," he wrote. "On the tables we found plates half-full of a by-now frozen soup which we devoured with an intense pleasure. . . ." It was January 22. As they departed, the SS had shot some of the prisoners.

"They killed them all methodically, with a shot in the nape of the neck, lining up their twisted bodies in the snow on the road; then they left." For the next seven days, Levi and his friends tried to find enough food to keep themselves alive. Many of the former prisoners died of disease and starvation. On January 27, Levi and a friend carried out one of their friends and put his body on the snow. Then the Russians arrived. Levi had been saved.[17]

As the Russians approached the concentration camp at Stutthof, Poland, Jews were forced to leave by the SS. They began a grueling march, dressed in rags, against the icy cold of winter. Henny Fletcher was one of the prisoners who participated in the march. "By then they knew, the Germans knew, that they had lost the war and that the Russians are on their tail," she said.

> They put us in a barn and . . . everybody was dying. . . . Every place, you sat next to a corpse. And one of my friends . . . came over to me and she said, "Henny, you still are walking around. Would you help me bury my mother?" And I helped her carry out her mother because that was the very, the first thing they [the SS] did is made us dig deep ditches because they knew. And I dropped the mother on a pile of bones. [Afterward] They closed the barn doors. . . . They poured gasoline around, all around, and they were going to burn the whole thing. Next thing . . . we hear banging on our . . . barn doors, and Russian spoken.[18]

After Auschwitz was liberated, Soviet soldiers found this warehouse filled with shoes and clothes from the victims who were killed at the camp. The Nazis intended to ship the goods to Germany where they would be used for the war effort.

The prisoners had been liberated just in time to escape death in the gas chambers.

At Chelmno, as the Russian armies approached the camp, the SS ordered the Jewish workers to level it. The barracks were destroyed and the crematoria were blown up. The SS wanted no evidence left behind of what had occurred there. Once the Jews had finished their work, the SS planned to kill them. One night, the SS called several Jews outside their barracks and shot them. Inside, Mordechai Zurawski knew that he would be next. "The SS man came in," he said later. "I hid behind the door—I had a knife in my hand; I jumped on the SS man and stabbed him. I broke his flashlight and stabbed right and left, and I escaped."[19]

In the west, Allied troops had entered Nazi-held Czechoslovakia and crossed the Rhine River in Germany. Alan Zimm was among the prisoners who were freed by the advancing armies. He recalled:

> you could see far away, the gate, opened up and a jeep with four military police, the English dressed up in the white belts and the white gloves and the red hats. . . . And a truck with loudspeakers behind them, and [one of the men] said, "My dear friends . . . you are free. You are liberated by the Allied forces. . . ."[20]

On April 4, American forces entered the labor camp at Ohrdruf, Germany. There they found four thousand people who had been killed as the Nazis fled. A week later, the Americans arrived at Buchenwald, where they found twenty-one thousand prisoners. Most of them were starving and looked like the walking dead. In addition there were mounds of dead bodies, people who had been killed at the camp. Earlier, thousands of Jews had been evacuated from Buchenwald by the SS guards. Some were shot along the way. The Nazis also abandoned Bergen-Belsen, after killing many of the inmates. But thousands of bodies were left unburied, where they were found by British troops liberating the camp. An epidemic of typhus had also broken out among the remaining prisoners. This disease, caused by bacteria, had already taken many lives at the camp. Even after Allied forces entered Bergen-Belsen, more prisoners continued to die.

Meanwhile, Himmler had ordered the destruction of the death camp at Dachau and the murder of all the prisoners so they could not "fall into enemy hands alive."[21] On April 20, as the Soviet armies entered Sachsenhausen death camp, they found only three thousand prisoners there. The rest had been forced to leave by the retreating SS. Many of the prisoners were shot by the guards because they were unable to march.

Berlin

As Russian troops approached Berlin, Hitler had holed up in his headquarters beneath the Chancellery—the seat of the Nazi government. Outside the building, the SS defended the Führer. Meanwhile, Himmler was still negotiating with the Allies. As historian Donald McKale wrote, "Like most Nazi leaders, Himmler now wanted to save his own skin. He realized the war was . . . lost and that Hitler would take Germany down . . . rather than capitulate. He hoped to show himself in as good a light as possible to the Allies and perhaps even play a role in a postwar Germany."[22] He also agreed to meet with Jewish leaders. On April 20, Himmler told them that none of the remaining camps would be destroyed, nor would any other Jewish prisoners be killed. As a result, Jewish women still held at Ravensbrück were released. Ten days later, the Russians entered the camp at Ravensbrück, which had been abandoned by the SS. Approximately thirty-three hundred prisoners were still there.

Realizing that the war was lost, Himmler tried to contact General Dwight Eisenhower, Supreme Allied Commander, to offer a German surrender. However, word of Himmler's activities leaked out. It was broadcast on the radio, and Hitler heard of it in his bunker. Furious with Himmler, the Führer ordered that he should be arrested. In a long document, Hitler also ordered that Himmler should be stripped of all his power and expelled from the Nazi party. On April 29, Hitler signed the document. The following day, he committed suicide.

10

The Legacy of Heinrich Himmler

In the document he left before his death, Adolf Hitler designated Admiral Karl Dönitz as his successor to lead the Third Reich. On May 8, 1945, however, Dönitz surrendered to the victorious Allies. World War II had ended in Europe.

Himmler, who had been disgraced by Hitler during his final days, was now on his own. He was a fugitive, the second most wanted man after Hitler, who was already dead. Himmler disguised himself as a policeman, named Heinrich Hitzinger. He had obtained Hitzinger's identity papers, after the man was arrested for disobeying orders. Himmler shaved his moustache and put a black patch over one eye to disguise himself. The former Nazi leader also removed his uniform and dressed in simple clothes so he would not be spotted.

For almost two weeks, Himmler moved from place to place, accompanied by some of his staff who were also disguised. It seemed relatively easy for them to go unnoticed.

Germany had been heavily bombed during the war. Many towns were strewn with rubble, and ordinary Germans were trying to do what they could to survive in the post-war ruins. No one had time to worry about Heinrich Himmler.

On May 21, however, Himmler, along with members of his staff, was picked up by a British patrol in northern Germany. He was wearing civilian clothes and a blue raincoat. Himmler and his associates were taken to another camp on May 23. Once inside the commander's office, Himmler removed his eye patch. He was instantly recognized and told his interrogators that he was indeed Heinrich Himmler. He was told to take off his clothes and searched. The British found a small case with a capsule of cyanide poison and a similar case that was empty. They assumed that Himmler had concealed the poison somewhere on his body, possibly inside his mouth.

The camp commander, Captain Thomas Selvester, said that Himmler "was quite prepared to talk, and indeed at times looked almost jovial. He looked ill when I first saw him but improved immensely after a meal and a wash. I found it impossible to believe that he could be the arrogant man portrayed by the press before and during the war."[1] Himmler was then taken to another interrogation center. There he was told to strip again. The British were afraid he might commit suicide before they could adequately question him, and they wanted to find the cyanide capsule. However, Himmler had hidden the capsule in a hole drilled inside one of his teeth. As the British forcefully opened his mouth to look for the capsule, Himmler bit it with his teeth. The cyanide capsule broke. Himmler died soon afterward—May 23, 1945.

The Architect of Genocide

As the man called the Architect of Genocide, Himmler had tried to execute Hitler's efforts to kill all the Jews in Europe.

More than 11 million had died, including 6 million Jews, as a result of the murders ordered by Himmler and committed by his henchmen. Yet the Reichsführer-SS hardly looked like a mass murderer. One of his colleagues said, "He looked to me like an intelligent elementary schoolteacher, certainly not a man of violence."[2] Himmler's SS officers often described him as someone who spoke like a professor, giving them fatherly advice in carrying out their duties.

However, those duties involved the murder of an entire group of people. Himmler had donned the military uniform of the Nazis and enthusiastically adopted the racism preached by Hitler. Perhaps, as his biographer Peter Padfield suggested, it started with Himmler's own feelings of inferiority. Himmler had been a poor athlete and he had been unable to serve in the armed forces during World War I. He made up for these things by taking on an important role in the Nazi party.[3] The fact that in his physical appearance he did not look like a true Nordic German may have also been one of the reasons that he became such a strong anti-Semite. Himmler also found in Hitler a leader whom he could follow. In turn, Hitler could rely on Himmler to be the most fanatical member of the SS. Himmler would stop at nothing to please his Führer—even mass murder.

By pleasing Hitler, Himmler quickly learned that he could achieve an important position in the Nazi party. Little by little, Himmler acquired more power until he was second only to Hitler, himself. Through his control of the SS, the Gestapo, and the death camps, Himmler controlled a powerful empire within the Third Reich. His men became Himmler's instruments, carrying out the Final Solution.

Ironically, Himmler himself became squeamish at the sight of death. He did not enjoy hunting, like many of the other

During a rally in 1934, Heinrich Himmler (left), Adolf Hitler (center), and Viktor Lutze, chief of staff of the SA, march between columns of Nazis. By 1945, Germany was defeated, the camps had been liberated, Lutze had died in a car crash, and both Hitler and Himmler had committed suicide.

Nazi leaders. He rarely attended a killing at one of his own death camps. And, when he did witness a shooting, it repulsed him. Nevertheless, he seemed to have no trouble ordering the deaths of millions.

Himmler also seemed to be a master at running a large organization, like the SS. As historian Hugh Thomas wrote:

> What is most disturbing about the way Himmler and everyone surrounding him went about their business is their insistence on observing the niceties of bureaucracy. They routinely spent hours deliberating on the minutiae of their horrendous acts, creating endless forms, lists and files to impose . . . order on the business of mass murder.[4]

One high-ranking member of the Nazi government once wrote: "Except for Hitler, no one is entirely without fear of Himmler . . . Himmler has built up the greatest power organization imaginable."[5] Himmler controlled the vast power of the SS. His agents were everywhere in the Third Reich; his Gestapo arrested innocent people at will; his soldiers murdered Jews in the streets; his SS guards took victims in the camps to their deaths by the hundreds of thousands. With this uncontrolled power at his fingertips, Himmler created the Holocaust—one of the darkest pages in human history.

TIMELINE

(Shaded areas indicate events in the life of Heinrich Himmler.)

1900

Heinrich Himmler is born.

1910

Himmler enters the gymnasium.

1914

World War I begins.

1918

Himmler joins the Eleventh Bavarian Infantry;
World War I ends; Germany is defeated.

1919

Himmler joins Freikorps Oberland.

1923

Himmler joins Reichsflagge, led by Ernst Röhm;

Himmler joins Nazi Party; Participates in Hitler's
Beer Hall Putsch in Munich.

1925

Himmler joins SS.

1927

Himmler is appointed Deputy Reichsführer-SS;

Marries Margaret Concerzowo.

1929

Himmler is named Reichsführer-SS;

Himmler's daughter, Gudrun, is born.

1933

Hitler becomes Chancellor of Germany.

March 22: Concentration camp at Dachau opens.

April 26: Gestapo established.

May 10: Nazis burn banned books in public.

1934

Himmler becomes head of Gestapo;
SS plays key role in the Night of the Long Knives.

August 2: Hitler names himself "Fuhrer," or leader,
of Germany.

1935

May 31: Jews in Germany no longer allowed to serve
in armed forces.

September 15: Anti-Jewish Nuremberg Laws are
enacted; Jews are no longer considered citizens of
Germany.

1936

Hitler appoints Himmler head of the police.

Nazis boycott Jewish-owned businesses.

March 7: Nazis occupy Rhineland.

July: Sachsenhausen concentration camp opens.

1937

July 15: Buchenwald concentration camp opens.

1938

Himmler enters Vienna during the Anschluss;
Jews are attacked in Germany and Austria during
Kristallnacht.

March: Mauthausen concentration camp opens.

March 13: Germany annexes Austria and applies all
anti-Jewish laws there.

July 6: League of Nations holds conference on Jewish
refugees at Evian, France, but no action is taken to
help the refugees.

October 5: All Jewish passports must now be
stamped with a red "J."

October 15: Nazi troops occupy the Sudentenland.

November 9-10: Kristallnacht, the Night of the Broken Glass; Jewish businesses and synagogues are destroyed and thirty thousand Jews are sent to concentration camps.

1939

Himmler accompanies Hitler into Prague, Czechoslovakia;

Hitler invades Poland; World War II begins;

SS begins killing Polish intellectuals and Jews.

March 15: Germans occupy Czechoslovakia.

August 23: Germany and the Soviet Union sign a non-aggression pact.

September 1: Germany invades Poland, beginning World War II.

October 28: First Polish ghetto established in Piotrkow.

November 23: Jews in Poland are forced to wear an arm band or yellow star.

1940

Polish Jews are moved into ghettos in major cities;

Himmler orders the construction of Auschwitz.

April 9: Germans occupy Denmark and southern Norway.

May 7: Lodz Ghetto is established.

May 20: Auschwitz concentration camp is established.

June 22: France surrenders to Germany.

September 27: Germany, Italy, and Japan form the Axis powers.

November 16: Warsaw Ghetto is established.

1941

Germany invades Russia; SS begins rounding up Jews inside Russian territory; Himmler designates Auschwitz to spearhead the Final Solution; Hitler gives Himmler full control of security measures in

1941 (continued)
the east; Jews massacred at Babi Yar near Kiev in Ukraine; Himmler orders massacre at Rumbula in Latvia.

June 22: Germany invades the Soviet Union.
October: Auschwitz II (Birkenau) death camp is established.

1942
Himmler visits death camps in eastern Europe, witnessing the murder of Jews.

January 20: Wannsee Conference in Berlin where the "Final Solution" is outlined.
March 17: Killings begin at Belzec death camp.
May: Killings begin at Sobibor death camp.
July22: Treblinka concentration camp is established.
Summer-Winter: Mass deportations to death camps begin.

1943
Nazis lose Battle of Stalingrad; war turns against Germany;
Himmler orders the destruction of the Warsaw ghetto;
Hitler appoints Himmler Interior Minister.

March: Liquidation of Krakow Ghetto begins.
April 19: Warsaw ghetto uprising.
Fall: Liquidation of Minsk, Vilna, and Riga ghettos.

1944
Himmler appointed by Hitler as Chief of German Armaments and Commander of the Home Army;
Himmler orders the destruction of Warsaw.

March 19: Germans invade and occupy Hungary; Eichmann arrives.

May 15: Jewish deportations from Hungary begin, most sent to Auschwitz.

June 24: Budapest Jews moved to yellow-star houses.

July 14: Soviet forces liberate Majdanek death camp.

October 20: Jewish draft for labor brigades begins.

November 2: Soviets break through defenses near Budapest; Jews in labor brigades massacred by Hungarian soldiers.

November 8: Death marches to Hegyeshalom begin.

December 8: Soviet siege of Budapest begins.

December 22: Eichmann attempts to assassinate Jewish Council; leaves Budapest.

December 24: Increased terrorism against Jews begins, including raids of legation offices, protected houses, children's homes, and hospitals.

1945

SS abandons concentration camps to Allies; Hitler commits suicide, as Russians attack Berlin; Himmler commits suicide after being captured.

Auschwitz inmates begin death march.

April 6–10: Buchenwald inmates sent on death march.

April 30: Hitler commits suicide.

May 8: Germany surrenders.

Chapter Notes

Chapter 1. A Meeting at Wannsee

1. Christopher Browning, *The Origins of the Final Solution* (Lincoln: University of Nebraska Press, 2004), p. 410.
2. Ibid., p. 353.
3. Martin Gilbert, *The Holocaust* (New York: Holt, Rinehart and Winston, 1985), p. 804
4. *Minutes of the Wannsee Conference*, n.d. <http://www.prorev.com/wannsee.htm> (October 26, 2004).
5. Peter Padfield, *Himmler* (New York: Henry Holt, 1990), p. 357. Excerpt from *Himmler* by Peter Padfield. Copyright © 1990 by Peter Padfield. Reprinted by permission of Henry Holt and Company, LLC.
6. *Minutes of the Wannsee Conference*.
7. Padfield, p. 357.
8. Gilbert, p. 283.

Chapter 2. Early Life and Anti-Semitism

1. Bradley F. Smith, *Heinrich Himmler: A Nazi in the Making, 1900–1926* (Stanford, Calif.: Hoover Institution Press, 1971), p. 20.
2. Ibid., p. 23.
3. Ibid., p. 25.
4. Ibid., p. 31.
5. Peter Padfield, *Himmler* (New York: Henry Holt, 1990), p. 24. Excerpt from *Himmler* by Peter Padfield. Copyright © 1990 by Peter Padfield. Reprinted by permission of Henry Holt and Company, LLC.
6. Smith, p. 34.
7. Padfield, p. 28.
8. Smith, pp. 50–52.
9. Padfield, p. 36.
10. Ibid., p. 42.
11. Smith, pp. 68–69.
12. Ibid., p. 69.
13. Padfield, p. 38.
14. Smith, pp. 74–75.
15. Ibid., p. 78.
16. Padfield, p. 42.
17. Smith, p. 89.

18. Padfield, p. 56.
19. Smith, p. 123.
20. Padfield, p. 55.
21. Smith, p. 122.

Chapter 3. Becoming a Nazi

1. Bradley F. Smith, *Heinrich Himmler: A Nazi in the Making, 1900–1926* (Stanford, Calif.: Hoover Institution Press, 1971), p. 142.

2. Ibid., pp. 142–143, Peter Padfield, *Himmler* (New York: Henry Holt, 1990), p. 68. Excerpt from *Himmler* by Peter Padfield. Copyright © 1990 by Peter Padfield. Reprinted by permission of Henry Holt and Company, LLC.

3. Michael Burleigh, *The Third Reich: A New History* (New York: Hill and Wang, 2000), pp. 91–92.

4. Padfield, pp. 89–90.

5. Ibid., p. 90.

6. Burleigh, p. 112.

7. Padfield, p. 99.

8. Smith, p. 172.

9. Padfield, p. 100.

10. Ibid., p. 115.

11. Ibid., p. 121.

Chapter 4. Chief of the German Police

1. Henry W. Mazal, "The Dachau Gas Chambers," *The Holocaust History Project*, February 7, 2001, <http://www.holocaust-history.org/dachau-gas-chambers/> (October 26, 2004).

2. George C. Browder, *Foundations of the Nazi Police State* (Lexington: The University of Kentucky Press, 1990), p. 67.

3. Ibid., p. 127.

4. Peter Padfield, *Himmler* (New York: Henry Holt, 1990), p. 138. Excerpt from *Himmler* by Peter Padfield. Copyright © 1990 by Peter Padfield. Reprinted by permission of Henry Holt and Company, LLC.

5. Ibid.

6. Ibid., p. 139.

7. Michael Burleigh, *The Third Reich: A New History* (New York: Hill and Wang, 2000), p. 194.

8. Ibid., pp. 196–197.

9. Ibid., p. 186.

10. Padfield, p. 159.
11. Ibid., p. 162.
12. Ibid., p. 164.
13. Joshua Greene and Shiva Kumar, eds., *Witness: Voices from the Holocaust* (New York: The Free Press, 2000), p. 11.
14. *The Nuremberg Laws on Citizenship and Race*, n.d., <http://www.mtsu.edu/~baustin/nurmlaw2.html> (October 26, 2004).
15. Padfield, p. 176.
16. Greene and Kumar, p. 13.
17. Ibid., pp. 25, 38, 39.
18. Burleigh, p. 303.
19. Padfield, p. 182.
20. Burleigh, p. 203.

Chapter 5. Persecuting Jews on Germany's Borders

1. John Roth and David Aretha, eds., *The Holocaust Chronicle* (Lincolnwood, Ill.: Publications International, Ltd., 2000), p. 137.
2. Peter Padfield, *Himmler* (New York: Henry Holt, 1990), p. 223. Excerpt from *Himmler* by Peter Padfield. Copyright © 1990 by Peter Padfield. Reprinted by permission of Henry Holt and Company, LLC.
3. Norman Davies, *Europe: A History* (New York: HarperCollins, 1996), p. 990.
4. Joshua Greene and Shiva Kumar, eds., *Witness: Voices from the Holocaust* (New York: The Free Press, 2000), pp. 37–38.
5. Michael Burleigh, *The Third Reich: A New History* (New York: Hill and Wang, 2000), p. 324.
6. Padfield, p. 240.
7. Ibid., p. 243.
8. Greene and Kumar, p. 28.
9. Burleigh, p. 330.
10. Ibid., p. 341.
11. Davies, p. 993.
12. Padfield, p. 245.
13. Davies, p. 997.
14. Ibid., p. 998.
15. Editors of Time-Life Books, *The SS* (Alexandria, Va.: Time-Life Books, 1989), pp. 109–110.
16. Ibid., pp. 110–111.
17. Burleigh, p. 442.

18. Greene and Kumar, p. 34.

19. Deborah Dwork and Robert Jan van Pelt, *Auschwitz: 1270 to the Present* (New York: Norton, 1996), pp. 158–159.

20. "Personal Histories, Ghettos," *USHMM*, n.d., <http://www.ushmm.org/museum/exhibit/online/phistories/phi_ghettos_ghetto ization_uu.htm> (October 26, 2004).

21. Richard Breitman, *The Architect of Genocide: Himmler and The Final Solution* (New York: Knopf, 1991), p. 81.

22. Editors of Time-Life Books, p. 118.

23. Dwork and Jan van Pelt, pp. 175–176.

24. Breitman, p. 121.

25. Ibid., pp. 125–126.

Chapter 6. Killing Jews in Russia

1. John Roth and David Aretha, eds., *The Holocaust Chronicle* (Lincolnwood, Ill.: Publications International, Ltd., 2000), p. 244.

2. "Personal Histories, Ghettos," *USHMM*, n.d., <http://www.ushmm.org/museum/exhibit/online/phistories/phi_ghettos_ghetto ization_uu.htm> (October 26, 2004).

3. Richard Rhodes, *Masters of Death: The SS-Einsatzgruppen and the Invention of the Holocaust* (New York: Knopf, 2002), p. 61.

4. Ibid., p. 44.

5. Ibid., p. 48.

6. Richard Breitman, *The Architect of Genocide: Himmler and The Final Solution* (New York: Knopf, 1991), p. 177.

7. Ibid., p. 176.

8. Ibid., p. 189.

9. Ibid., p. 193.

10. Rhodes, pp. 101–104.

11. Peter Padfield, *Himmler* (New York: Henry Holt, 1990), p. 343. Excerpt from *Himmler* by Peter Padfield. Copyright © 1990 by Peter Padfield. Reprinted by permission of Henry Holt and Company, LLC.

12. Rhodes, p. 139.

13. Ibid., p. 215.

14. Padfield, p. 354.

15. Rhodes, p. 200.

16. Christopher Browning, *The Origins of the Final Solution* (Lincoln: University of Nebraska Press, 2004), p. 313.

17. Yitzhak Arad, *Belzec, Sobibor, Treblinka: The Operation Reinhard Death Camps* (Bloomington: Indiana University Press, 1987), p. 24.

18. Claude Lanzmann, *Shoah: An Oral History of the Holocaust* (New York: Pantheon Books, 1985), p. 6.

19. Arad, p. 24.

20. Martin Gilbert, *The Holocaust* (New York: Holt, Rinehart and Winston, 1985), p. 268.

Chapter 7. Architect of the Holocaust

1. John Roth and David Aretha, eds., *The Holocaust Chronicle* (Lincolnwood, Ill.: Publications International, Ltd., 2000), p. 295.

2. Yitzhak Arad, *Belzec, Sobibor, Treblinka: The Operation Reinhard Death Camps* (Bloomington: Indiana University Press, 1987), p. 63.

3. Ibid., p. 65.

4. Ibid., p. 183.

5. Ibid., pp. 70–71.

6. Ibid., p. 76.

7. Roth and Aretha, p. 340.

8. Richard Rhodes, *Masters of Death: The SS-Einsatzgruppen and the Invention of the Holocaust* (New York: Knopf, 2002), pp. 254–255.

9. Roth and Aretha, p. 282.

10. David Hackett, *The Buchenwald Report* (Boulder, Colo.: Westview Press, 1995), p. 51.

11. Peter Padfield, *Himmler* (New York: Henry Holt, 1990), p. 392. Excerpt from *Himmler* by Peter Padfield. Copyright © 1990 by Peter Padfield. Reprinted by permission of Henry Holt and Company, LLC.

12. Louis Bülow, "Hell of Sobibor Deathcamp," *The Holocaust Crimes, Heroes, and Villains,* © 2004–2006, <http://www.auschwitz.dk/Sobibor.htm> (October 26, 2004).

13. Padfield, p. 400.

14. Claude Lanzmann, *Shoah: An Oral History of the Holocaust* (New York: Pantheon Books, 1985), p. 47.

15. Ibid., pp. 53, 55.

16. Martin Gilbert, *The Holocaust* (New York: Holt, Rinehart and Winston, 1985), p. 239.

17. Arad, p. 186.

18. Gilbert, p. 249.

19. Rhodes, p. 255.

20. Gilbert, p. 286.

Chapter 8. Himmler Increases the Jewish Terror

1. Michael Burleigh, *The Third Reich: A New History* (New York: Hill and Wang, 2000), p. 508.

2. Donald McKale, *Hitler's Shadow War: The Holocaust and World War II* (New York: Cooper Square Press, 2002), p. 308.

3. Ibid., p. 309.

4. Louis Bülow, "Bergen-Belsen: KZ Camp," *The Holocaust Crimes, Heroes, and Villains,* © 2004–2006, <http://www.auschwitz.dk/Bergenbelsen.htm> (October 26, 2004).

5. "Sachsenhausen," n.d., <http://www.jewishgen.org/Forgotten Camps/Camps/SachsenhausenEng.html> (October 26, 2004).

6. *Chelmno Extermination Camp,* n.d., <http://weber.ucsd.edu/~lzamosc/gchelmno.html> (October 26, 2004).

7. McKale, pp. 313–314.

8. Joshua Greene and Shiva Kumar, eds., *Witness: Voices from the Holocaust* (New York: The Free Press, 2000), p. 72.

9. Peter Padfield, *Himmler* (New York: Henry Holt, 1990), p. 457. Excerpt from *Himmler* by Peter Padfield. Copyright © 1990 by Peter Padfield. Reprinted by permission of Henry Holt and Company, LLC.

10. McKale, p. 316.

11. Padfield, p. 447.

12. "Honoring Mordecai Anielewicz," *Simon Wiesenthal Center Multimedia Learning Center Online,* n.d., <http://motlc.wiesenthal.com/text/x01/xr0171.html> (October 26, 2004).

13. McKale, p. 319.

14. Yitzhak Arad, *Belzec, Sobibor, Treblinka: The Operation Reinhard Death Camps* (Bloomington: Indiana University Press, 1987), pp. 270–280.

15. Ibid., pp. 297–298.

16. Ibid., p. 327.

17. McKale, p. 331.

18. Ibid., chap. 22.

19. Judith Jaegermann, "Memories of My Childhood in the Holocaust," *Remember.org,* n.d., <http://remember.org/witness/jagermann.html> (October 26, 2004).

20. Deborah Dwork and Robert Jan van Pelt, *Auschwitz: 1270 to the Present* (New York: Norton, 1996), p. 351.

21. Claude Lanzmann, *Shoah: An Oral History of the Holocaust* (New York: Pantheon Books, 1985), p. 59.

22. Joachim Fest, "Heinrich Himmler—Petty Bourgeois and Grand Inquisitor," *The Face of the Third Reich*, n.d., <http://www.ourcivi lisation.com/smartboard/shop/festjc/chap9.htm> (October 26, 2004).

Chapter 9. Last Year in Power

1. Martin Gilbert, *The Holocaust* (New York: Holt, Rinehart and Winston, 1985), p. 656.

2. Adolf Eichmann, "I Transported Them . . . To the Butcher," *The Einsatzgruppen*, May 29, 1998, <http://www.einsatzgruppenarchives. com/trials/profiles/eichmannintro.html> (October 26, 2004).

3. Ibid.

4. Deborah Dwork and Robert Jan van Pelt, *Auschwitz: 1270 to the Present* (New York: Norton, 1996), pp. 340, 342.

5. Gilbert, pp. 687–688.

6. Ibid., p. 665.

7. Dwork and Jan van Pelt, p. 327.

8. John Roth and David Aretha, eds., *The Holocaust Chronicle* (Lincolnwood, Ill.: Publications International, Ltd., 2000), p. 507.

9. Peter Padfield, *Himmler* (New York: Henry Holt, 1990), p. 501. Excerpt from *Himmler* by Peter Padfield. Copyright © 1990 by Peter Padfield. Reprinted by permission of Henry Holt and Company, LLC.

10. Hugh Thomas, *The Strange Death of Heinrich Himmler* (New York: St. Martin's Press, 2001), pp. 53–55.

11. Padfield, p. 524.

12. Thomas, p. 103.

13. Padfield, p. 523.

14. Ibid., p. 544.

15. Dwork and Jan van Pelt, p. 9.

16. Gilbert, p. 772.

17. Primo Levi, *Survival in Auschwitz* (New York: Macmillan, 1960), pp. 157–173.

18. Personal Histories, "Liberation," *USHMM*, n.d., <http://www. ushmm.org/museum/exhibit/online/phistories/phi_liberation_ encounter_uu.htm> (October 26, 2004).

19. Gilbert, p. 770.

20. Personal Histories, "Liberation."

21. Padfield, p. 582.

22. Donald McKale, *Hitler's Shadow War: The Holocaust and World War II* (New York: Cooper Square Press, 2002), p. 383.

Chapter 10. The Legacy of Heinrich Himmler

1. Hugh Thomas, *The Strange Death of Heinrich Himmler* (New York: St. Martin's Press, 2001), p. 155.

2. Ibid., p. 14.

3. Peter Padfield, *Himmler* (New York: Henry Holt, 1990), p. 552.

4. Thomas, p. 15.

5. Ibid.

Glossary

Anschluss—Refers to Adolf Hitler's takeover of Austria in 1938 and its annexation into the Third Reich.

anti-Semitism—Prejudice against Jewish people that formed a central principle of Nazi policy during the 1930s and 1940s, leading to the Holocaust.

blitzkrieg—A German word that means lightning war and refers to the tactics used in rapid Nazi victories in Poland and Western Europe during 1939 and 1940.

Case White—The secret name for the Nazi invasion of Poland in 1939.

Case Yellow—This secret code name was used by the Nazis for their invasion of western Europe in 1940.

death camps—The name given to concentration camps, such as Sobibor, Majdanek, Treblinka, Auschwitz, Belzec, and Chelmno, that were established by the SS to execute the Final Solution.

Death's Head—Units of the SS that served as concentration camp guards.

Einsatzgruppen—Units of the SS that followed the German troops in the invasion of Russia in 1941 and were ordered to shoot Jews, leading Bolsheviks, and other "enemies" of the Nazi government.

Final Solution—In German, *Endlösung*, a Nazi term that refers to the murder of the entire Jewish population of Europe.

Führer—A term that means leader; used by Adolf Hitler.

Gauleiter—A regional Nazi political leader in Germany.

General Government—The area of western and central Poland ruled by the Nazis after their invasion of 1939.

genocide—Term that refers to the destruction of an entire group of people classified in a common way.

Gestapo—The name of the Nazi Secret State Police, controlled by Heinrich Himmler as part of the SS.

ghetto—The area of a city in Europe where Jews had been forced to live since the Middle Ages; Nazis drove Jews into ghettos in major cities of eastern Europe, where they were killed or taken to the death camps.

gymnasium—The name for a German high school.

Holocaust—A Greek word, meaning "burnt offering," which refers to the liquidation of European Jews by the Nazis during the 1930s and 1940s.

Kapo—A Jewish leader of the Sonderkommandos whom the Nazis employed at the death camps to carry on a variety of tasks, including the job of taking bodies to the crematoria.

Lebensraum—A term that means "living space" and a major justification used by Adolf Hitler to invade Poland and Russia—to provide more living space for the German people.

liquidate—To do away with.

Madagascar Plan—A program considered by the Nazis that would have involved shipping thousands of Jews out of Europe to Madagascar in eastern Africa.

Nazi—Abbreviation that refers to the National Socialist German Workers' Party, led by Adolf Hitler.

Operation Barbarossa—The code name for the Nazi invasion of the Soviet Union in 1941.

Operation Reinhard—Named after Reinhard Heydrich—Himmler's chief of staff—it referred to the building of new death camps in Poland, including Sobibor, Treblinka, and Belzec, and the murder of Jews at these camps.

pogrom—A term that refers to an organized, violent attack on Jews.

Reichstag—The name for the German Parliament.

SD—The Nazi Security Service headed by Reinhard Heydrich under the direction of Heinrich Himmler.

SS—The Schutzstaffel—Hitler's elite guard—it was directed by Reichsführer-SS Heinrich Himmler and later expanded by him to include a large empire of spies, police, soldiers, and concentration camp guards.

Sonderkommandos—Jewish work teams in death camps that were forced to participate in the mass killings of Jews.

Third Reich—Name used by the Nazis to describe their regime, which lasted from 1933 to 1945.

Zyklon B—Pesticide that was used to kill insects and rodents and later employed in the death camps to kill Jews.

Further Reading

Books on Heinrich Himmler

Breitman, Richard. *The Architect of Genocide: Himmler and the Final Solution.* New York: Knopf, 1991.

Padfield, Peter. *Himmler.* New York: Henry Holt, 1990.

Books on the Holocaust

Anflick, Charles. *Resistance: Teen Partisans and Resisters Who Fought Nazi Tyranny.* New York: Rosen Publishing Group, 1999.

Bauer, Yehuda. *A History of the Holocaust.* New York: Franklin Watts, 2001.

Boas, Jacob, ed. *We Are Witnesses: Five Diaries of Teenagers Who Died in the Holocaust.* New York: Scholastic, 1996.

Croci, Pascal. *Auschwitz.* New York: Harry N. Abrams, 2004.

Dwork, Deborah and Robert Jan van Pelt. *Auschwitz, 1270 to the Present.* New York: Norton, 1996.

_____. *Holocaust: A History.* New York: Norton, 2002.

Koestler-Grack, Rachel A. *The Story of Anne Frank.* Philadelphia: Chelsea Clubhouse, 2004.

Levine, Karen. *Hana's Suitcase: A True Story.* Morton Grove, Ill.: Albert Whitman, 2003.

Rogasky, Barbara. *Smoke and Ashes: The Story of the Holocaust.* New York: Holiday House, 2002.

Roth, John, and David Aretha, eds. *The Holocaust Chronicle.* Lincolnwood, Ill.: Publications International, Ltd., 2000.

Sherrow, Victoria. *The Blaze Engulfs: January 1939–December 1941.* Woodbridge, Conn.: Blackbirch Press, 1998.

Books on the Nazis and the Nazi Regime

Ayer, Eleanor. *Adolf Hitler.* San Diego: Lucent Books, 1996.

Bartoletti, Susan Campbell. *Hitler Youth: Growing Up in Hitler's Shadow.* New York: Scholastic, 2004.

Bauer, Yehuda. *Jews for Sale? Nazi-Jewish Negotiations, 1933–1945.* New Haven: Yale University Press, 1994.

Browning, Christopher. *The Origins of the Final Solution: The Evolution of Nazi Jewish Policy, September 1939–March 1942.* Lincoln: University of Nebraska Press, 2003.

Burleigh, Michael. *The Third Reich: A New History.* New York: Hill and Wang, 2000.

Cartlidge, Cherese, and Charles Clark. *Life of a Nazi Soldier.* San Diego, Calif.: Lucent Books, 2001.

Evans, Richard. *The Coming of the Third Reich.* New York: Penguin Press, 2003.

Giblin, James. *The Life and Death of Adolf Hitler.* New York: Clarion Books, 2002.

Hackett, David. *The Buchenwald Report.* Boulder, Colo.: Westview Press, 1995.

Höss, Rudolf. *Death Dealer: The Memoirs of the SS Kommandant at Auschwitz.* New York: Prometheus Books, 1992.

Knopp, Guido. *Hitler's Henchmen.* New York: Sutton, 2000.

McKale, Donald. *Hitler's Shadow War: The Holocaust and World War II.* New York: Cooper Square Press, 2002.

Rhodes, Richard. *Masters of Death: The SS Einsatzgruppen and the Invention of the Holocaust.* New York: Knopf, 2002.

Sachs, Ruth. *Adolf Eichmann: Engineer of Death.* New York: Rosen Pub. Group, 2001.

Schneider, Helga. *Let Me Go,* trans. Shaun Whiteside. New York: Walker & Co., 2004.

Wistrich, Robert. *Hitler and the Holocaust.* New York: Modern Library, 2001.

Books on Survivors

Altman, Linda Jacobs. *Simon Wiesenthal.* San Diego, Calif: Lucent Books, 2000.

Axelrod, Toby. *Hans and Sophie Scholl: German Resisters of the White Rose.* New York: Rosen Pub. Group, 2001.

Ayer, Eleanor. *In The Ghettos: Teens Who Survived the Ghettos of the Holocaust.* New York: Rosen Publishing Group, 1999.

Britton-Jackson, Livia. *I Have Lived a Thousand Years: Growing Up in the Holocaust.* New York: Simon and Schuster Books for Young Readers, 1997.

Currie, Stephen. *Escapes from Nazi Persecution.* San Diego, Calif.: Lucent Books, 2004.

Holocaust Memories: Speaking the Truth in Their Own Voices. New York: Franklin Watts, 2001.

Lewis, Mark, and Jacob Frank. *Himmler's Jewish Tailor: The Story of Holocaust Survivor Jacob Frank.* Syracuse, N.Y.: Syracuse University Press, 2000.

McCann, Michelle R. *Luba: The Angel of Bergen-Belsen.* As told by Luba Tryszynska-Frederick. Berkeley, Calif.: Tricycle Press, 2003.

Shuter, Jane. *Resistance to the Nazis.* Chicago: Heinemann Library, 2003.

Smith, Frank Dabba. *Elsie's War: A Story of Courage in Nazi Germany.* London: Frances Lincoln, 2004.

Wartenburg, Marion Yorck von. *The Power of Solitude: My Life in the German Resistance,* trans. and ed. Julie M. Winter. Lincoln, NE: University of Nebraska Press, 2000.

Wiesel, Elie. *Night.* New York: Bantam, 1982.

Zapruder, Alexandra, ed. *Salvaged Pages: Young Writers' Diaries of the Holocaust.* New Haven: Yale University Press, 2002.

Internet Addresses

Jewish Virtual Library: Heinrich Himmler
<http://www.jewishvirtuallibrary.org>

> *Click on "The Library" at the left. Select "Biography."*
> *Scroll down and click on "Heinrich Himmler."*

Minutes of the Wannsee Conference
<http://www.historyplace.com>

> *Scroll down and click on "Holocaust Timeline" under the*
> *"Nazi Germany/World War II" heading. Scroll down and click*
> *on "Wannsee Conference to coordinate the 'Final Solution.'"*
> *under the "1942" heading.*

The United States Holocaust Memorial Museum: Introduction to the Holocaust.
<http://www.ushmm.org>

> *Click on "Introduction to the Holocaust" at the left.*

Index

A

Anielewicz, Mordecai, 112–113
anti-Semitism, 25, 27, 28, 30, 33–34, 40, 137
Aryan, 33, 35, 47, 53, 69, 73, 75
Auschwitz (death camp), 76, 81, 91, 96–97, 98, 100, 104, 116, 117, 118–119, 120, 121, 122, 126, 127–128, 129
Austria, 17, 19, 21, 61–62, 64, 65, 66, 69, 75, 98, 103, 107, 121

B

Bavaria, 16–17, 18, 19, 22, 25, 26, 27, 31, 32, 33, 34, 43, 45, 46, 58
Beer Hall Putsch, 32
Belzec (death camp), 87, 89, 91, 93–94, 95, 96, 100, 104, 114
Bergen-Belsen (concentration camp), 106, 132–133
Birkenau (concentration camp), 97, 116, 118
Buchenwald (concentration camp), 58–59, 98, 132

C

Chelmno (death camp), 14, 89, 91, 92-93, 109–110, 111, 124, 132
Churchill, Winston, 65, 77
Communists, 11, 23, 25, 26, 27, 37, 39, 40, 42, 43, 56, 61, 72, 78, 79, 126, 129
concentration camps, 13, 14, 43, 45, 46, 56, 58–59, 60, 61–62, 66, 68, 70, 76, 87, 89, 91, 95, 106, 116, 120, 128. See also Bergen-Belsen; Birkenau; Buchenwald; Chelmno; Dachau; Final Solution; Flossenburg; Gas chambers; Mauthausen; Poniatowa labor camp; Ravensbrück; Sachsenhausen; Stutthof; Theresienstadt.
Concerzowo, Margaret ("Marga"), 35, 48, 52, 125
Czechoslovakia, 59, 64–66, 69, 75, 97, 116, 127, 132

D

Dachau (concentration camp), 43, 45, 58, 61–62, 72, 81, 117, 133
death camps, 13, 80, 81, 83, 89, 93, 95, 96, 98, 100, 101, 102, 104, 105, 106, 107, 110, 111, 112, 113, 116, 118, 121, 122, 126, 127, 133, 137, 139. See also Auschwitz; Belzec; Chelmno, Majdanek, Sobibor, Treblinka.
Depression, 37

E

Eichmann, Adolf, 14, 58, 77, 116, 120, 121
Einsatzgruppen, 70, 79, 80, 84, 85, 86, 87

F

Final Solution (Endlösung), 10–11, 13–15, 81–82, 87, 92, 101, 115, 121, 123, 137. See also Holocaust.
Flossenburg (concentration camp), 58
Freemasons, 56, 58

G

gas chambers, 11, 14, 87, 89, 91, 92, 94, 96, 100, 101, 102, 107, 116, 117, 118, 120, 122, 127, 128
gas trucks, 89, 91, 93, 104, 109, 110

Gestapo, 43, 46, 50, 55, 56, 58, 59, 65, 66, 128, 137, 139
ghettoes, 13, 74–75, 79, 80–81, 84, 89, 93, 98, 102, 110, 111–113, 116, 121, 127
Globocnik, Odilo, 92, 93, 95
Göring, Hermann, 11, 42, 43, 46, 82
Grynszpan, Herschel, 66, 68

H

Heinrich, Prince, 17, 18, 22
Heydrich, Reinhard, 11, 13, 14, 39, 40, 43, 50, 51, 56, 61, 62, 64, 65, 70, 72, 82, 92, 96, 97, 98, 100, 121
Himmler, Gebhard (brother), 22, 27
Himmler, Gebhard (father), 16, 17, 18, 19, 27, 28, 38, 69
Himmler, Heinrich
    anti-Semitism, 11, 27, 28, 30, 33, 137
    becomes leader of the SS, 35
    betrayal of Adolf Hitler, 124, 128–129, 133–134
    birth, 16, 18
    capture, 136
    childhood, 18–19, 21
    children, 35, 48, 125
    death, 136
    education, 18–19, 23, 26, 27, 28, 30
    farm work, 26–27
    medical problems, 69–70, 82, 83, 112
    military service, 21, 22–23
    Nazi party membership, 31–35, 37–39, 41
Himmler, Konrad, 16, 19
Hindenburg, Paul von, 41, 45, 51
Hitler, Adolf, 10, 11, 30, 31, 32, 33–34, 35, 37–39, 41, 42, 45, 46, 48–49, 50, 51, 52, 56, 61, 64, 65, 66, 68, 69, 70, 72, 73, 77, 78, 80, 81–82, 85, 87, 89, 105, 106, 115,

119, 124, 125, 126, 128, 133, 134, 135, 136, 137, 139
Holocaust, 15, 92, 122, 139. *See also* Final Solution.
Höss, Rudolf, 76, 81, 91, 96, 100, 117, 121

J

Jews,
    medical experimentation on, 97, 122
    murder of, 62, 67, 72, 75–76, 79, 81, 82, 84, 85, 86–87, 89, 91, 92–94, 96–98, 100–102, 103, 104, 105–107, 109–111, 112–113, 114, 115–116, 117, 118–119, 120, 121, 122–124, 127, 128, 129, 131, 132, 133, 136–137, 139. *See also* death camps; Final Solution; Holocaust.
    persecution of, 13, 34, 43, 52–53, 55, 58–60, 64, 65–66, 73, 74, 75, 76–77, 79–80. *See also* concentration camps; Kristallnacht.
    revolts by, 110–111, 112–115, 127–128

K

Kristallnacht, 66–68

L

Levi, Primo, 129, 131
Lodz, Poland, 74, 75, 89, 93, 109, 127

M

Majdanek (death camp), 87, 100, 116, 126
Mauthausen (concentration camp), 62, 81, 107
Mein Kampf, 33
Mengele, Josef, 118, 122

N

National Socialist Workers' Party. *See* Nazi Party.

Nazi Party,
beginning of, 30, 31–33
rise to power of, 34, 37, 38, 41, 42, 51–52

Nebe, Arthur, 82, 85

Night of Blood, 102, 104

Night of Long Knives, 50–51, 82

Nuremberg Laws, 52–53

O

Operation Barbarossa, 78

Operation Nursemaid, 75

Operation Reinhard, 100

P

Poland, 13, 14, 59, 69–70, 71, 72, 73–76, 78, 79, 80, 87, 89, 100, 104, 110, 111, 115, 123, 124, 131

Poniatowa (concentration camp), 115

Potthast, Hedwig, 125

R

Rath, Ernst vom, 66

Ravensbrück (concentration camp), 68, 109, 133

Reichstag, 32, 37, 41, 42, 68

Röhm, Ernst, 30, 32, 39, 43, 50–51

Russia, 78–80, 81, 82, 84, 85, 86–87, 89, 91, 105, 126

Russian Army. *See* Soviet Army.

S

SA (storm troopers), 32, 39, 41, 43, 50, 51, 52

Sachsenhausen (concentration camp), 58, 59, 68, 107

Schutzstaffel (SS),
beginning of, 34–35
racial purity of, 35, 52, 62
training of, 48–49

SD. *See* Sicherheitsdienst.

Sicherheitsdienst (SD), 39, 50–51, 55, 56, 58, 59, 60

Sobibor (death camp), 93, 95, 96, 100, 103, 111, 114–115, 116

Sonderkommandos, 94, 100, 118, 127

Soviet Army, 105, 120, 123, 125, 126, 127, 129, 132, 133

Soviet Union, 11, 13, 25, 70, 78, 87, 105, 107, 126, 129

SS. *See* Schutzstaffel.

Stalin, Joseph, 78, 127

Stangl, Franz, 103

Stauffenberg, Klaus von, 124, 126

Strasser, Gregor, 33, 34, 51

Stroop, Jürgen, 112, 113

Stutthof (concentration camp), 131

T

T–4, 85, 89

Theresienstadt (concentration camp), 98, 116, 127

Treaty of Versailles, 27, 30

Treblinka (death camp), 93, 95, 100, 101–102, 103, 104, 110, 111, 112, 113, 115, 116, 117

W

Wannsee conference, 10–11, 13–15, 92, 121

Warsaw, Poland, 13, 72, 74, 76, 93, 96, 102, 104, 110, 111–113, 114, 126–127, 128

Weimar Republic, 23, 25, 31, 30, 33, 39

Wirth, Christian, 92, 94, 95, 103

World War I, 11, 19, 20, 21, 22–23, 27, 38, 41, 47, 58, 65, 69, 95, 117, 137

Z

Zipperer, Wolfgang Falk, 20

Zyklon B, 91, 93